# A KUT PRISONER

KASTAMUNI

THE CASTLE ROCK (KASTAMUNI)

# A KUT PRISONER

### By H. C. W. BISHOP

**The Naval & Military Press Ltd**

in association with

**The National Army Museum, London**

*Published jointly by*

## The Naval & Military Press Ltd

Unit 10 Ridgewood Industrial Park,
Uckfield, East Sussex,
TN22 5QE England

Tel: +44 (0) 1825 749494
Fax: +44 (0) 1825 765701

www.naval-military-press.com
www.military-genealogy.com
www.militarymaproom.com

*and*

## The National Army Museum, London

www.national-army-museum.ac.uk

Printed and bound in Great Britain by
CPI Antony Rowe, Chippenham and Eastbourne

*In reprinting in facsimile from the original, any imperfections are inevitably reproduced
and the quality may fall short of modern type and cartographic standards.*

TO THE MEMORY OF ALL THOSE BRITISH
AND INDIAN OFFICERS AND MEN OF
THE KUT GARRISON WHO HAVE SUF-
FERED AND DIED IN CAPTIVITY THIS
BOOK IS REVERENTLY DEDICATED

# INTRODUCTION

THE experiences related in the following pages are simply the individual fortunes of a subaltern of the Indian Army Reserve of Officers who had his first taste of fighting at the battle of Ctesiphon, and was afterwards taken prisoner by the Turks with the rest of the Kut Garrison, ultimately succeeding in escaping from Asia Minor. It is not intended to generalize in any way, since an individual, unless of exalted rank, sees as a rule only his own small environment and cannot pretend to speak for the majority of his comrades.

The book is published in the hope that it may prove of interest to the many relatives and friends of the Kut prisoners.

Acknowledgments are due to Messrs. Blackwood, the *Times of India*, and the *Pioneer* for their kind permission to republish those chapters which originally appeared in these papers.

# CONTENTS

# LIST OF ILLUSTRATIONS

# A KUT PRISONER

# A KUT PRISONER

## CHAPTER I

### CTESIPHON

IN India, in the early days of the war, a newly gazetted subaltern of the Indian Army Reserve of Officers was sent for a month's preliminary training to one of the few remaining British regular battalions. Afterwards he was attached to an Indian Regiment, and, if fortunate, went on service with the same battalion. A great number, however, were sent off to join other units in the field. In this way I found myself arriving in Basra on October 2nd, 1915, with a draft for a regiment[1] of whom I had known nothing a few days before leaving India. However, the "Nobody's Child" feeling was very soon a thing of the past, and I was welcomed by a mess full of the best comrades any fellow could desire.

The battle of Es-Sinn had just taken

---

[1] The 66th Punjabis.

place, and the 6th Division under General Townshend were then following the Turks up the Tigris above Kut. Our own fortune appeared to be to remain in Basra as part of the garrison ; but, much to every one's delight, different news came a week or two later and on the 25th October we set off up stream, hoping to get right through to the front but with some fear that we might be kept at Amara.

In those days travelling up the Tigris took a long time, and we spent a fortnight in reaching Azizie, a journey which can now be accomplished mostly by rail in two days.

The regiment was accommodated on two of the river steamers, each having two big barges lashed alongside. The current is considerable and the heavily weighted steamer could only advance very slowly. In many places the river becomes very narrow, especially between Kurna and Amara, and much time was spent in bumping into sand-banks and struggling to get clear.

We made short halts at Kurna, Amara, and Kut, the latter striking one as a horribly dusty and dirty little Arab town. Every night we used to tie up to the bank, as navigation by night was too risky with so little water in the river. On the last stretch to Azizie, we were warned to be on the alert for Arab snipers, and great preparations were made accordingly. A few shots were fired next morning, but nothing more than one Arab in the distance was seen. Other boats and convoys coming up had a much more lively time from raiding parties of the local tribes.

Azizie was reached in the afternoon, and presented a scene of the greatest activity. The village itself consisted of only a few mud huts, but for some distance along the dusty bank of the river General Townshend's force was concentrated. Nothing could be a greater contrast to the deserted stretches of country through which we had passed than the bustle and life of a force about to advance.

A few days later—on Monday, November 15th—the whole of the 6th Division and attached troops were on the march for Bagdad, the first stage being El Kutunie, some seven miles only. Here three days were spent and the final preparations completed. There was a little sniping at night from the further bank of the river, but this was quickly dealt with by the *Firefly*, the first of the new monitors to come into commission on the river.

Great excitement prevailed on the night

of the 18th when it was suddenly reported that the whole Turkish Force, which considerably outnumbered our own, was on the march to attack us and was expected to arrive and commence hostilities before morning. We spent a very industrious night, digging feverishly and wondering when the enemy would turn up.

Morning arrived, to find many trenches but no sign of the Turks, and we later found that the previous reports had been entirely misleading. However, fresh orders were soon received, and not long after daybreak the whole force was off again, split into various columns whose mission was to encompass and annihilate the Turkish advance troops at Zeur, about ten miles further on. However, the enemy eluded us, as he had done previously, and got away just in time. After doing several miles across country in attack formation, always expecting to hear firing beginning in front, we found we had arrived in the position the Turks had just vacated.

Next day a short march brought us to Lajj, a small hamlet on the river which was to be our jumping-off place for the forthcoming battle, and, as we believed, triumphal march on to Bagdad. All except the minimum of kit had been left at Azizie, whence it was to follow by steamer to Bagdad as soon as might be.

Before leaving Azizie, the general had given all senior officers some idea of the problem we had to tackle, and they realized it would be no walk-over. The rest of us, fortunately, thought only of a repetition of the former successes, and that we should enjoy a cheerful Christmas in Bagdad.

Detailed maps had been issued, not only of the Turks' position at Ctesiphon, but also of Bagdad and the methods to be adopted to push the enemy through and out of the city.

At Lajj we were about nine miles from the Arch of Ctesiphon, built by Chosroes I. in the 6th cent. B.C. and round which battles had been fought from time immemorial. From the top of a sand-dune near general headquarters, the magnificent ruin was clearly visible standing up gaunt and alone above the flat plain. The Turks' position surrounded the Arch and stretched back on both banks of the river.

We bivouacked one night at Lajj and at nine o'clock the following evening—Sunday, November 21st—the final advance began.

Our plan was to surround and defeat the Turks on the left bank, where the greater

part of their forces lay, and to drive them back
on the Tigris or Diala River.

The force was split into four columns,
which were to attack from different angles,
the " Flying " column being deputed to complete the victory by dashing on to Bagdad
and seizing the Bagdad end of the Samarra
Railway.

At midnight we reached our station on
some sand-hills about four to five miles due
east of the Arch, which we could see very
clearly as soon as it became light. It was a
bitterly cold night and after digging in we
lay down to get what sleep we could before
dawn broke.

The attack was to be begun by the
columns further north, who had had a
longer march and were further round the
Turkish flank.

There appeared to be considerable delay
on their part, and it was an hour after the
advertised time when our advance began.
In the meantime a troop of Turkish cavalry
had come out on a reconnaissance, but had
thought better of coming up as far as our
sand-hills and, after hesitating, retired un-
molested by us.

As we debouched from the high ground,
we could see masses of Turks, apparently

retiring in orderly formation towards their second line or still further, and the thought occurred that they were not going to wait even for us to attack. Actually, however, these were troops from the other side of the river being hastily brought across to strengthen the Turkish reserves opposite to us.

Our particular destination was a point marked V. P. on our map, and understood to be the " Vital Point " of the Turkish line. It fell quickly to our attack, but was not carried at a light cost, and, still worse, was not so all-essential to the Turkish resistance as it should have been. Our advance was held up on the Turkish second line and, unfortunately, we were not powerful or numerous enough to break this also. The Turks had a fine position and their trenches were sighted with the greatest skill. Aided by the mirage effect, it was almost impossible to discern these trenches until right upon them ; we, on the other hand, were out in the open plain, which was as flat as a billiard table and offered no cover of any sort. The Turkish front line was protected with barbed wire, and had they been provided with more machine-guns and been prepared to see things out a little longer, we should have fared very badly. As it was, we lost heavily in taking

V. P. and the adjacent trench lines, and were too crippled to do much more.

In the afternoon the Turks counter-attacked ; but our guns were too much for them, and they gained nothing.

Evening found a confused force bivouacked round V. P. There were dreadful gaps in all ranks. About midnight I found my way back to my own battalion, to discover the colonel and M. O., the only two officers still carrying on. One other subaltern besides myself had been posted away from the regiment during the day, but, of the rest, only two were left out of ten who had gone into action with the battalion that morning. Other regiments were in much the same state, and it was evident that we had suffered terribly and had not completely smashed the enemy. Later on we heard that our casualties had reached a total of nearly 5,000, while the Turks were said to have lost twice this figure.

The next morning we took up our position along the Turks' old front line, and no more fighting took place until the afternoon, when the Turks came back once more. Attacks followed during the night and prospects were considered anything but rosy for us by those in authority. However, the Turks had had enough, and by next morning were again out of range.

It was imperative for us now to get closer to the river for water, and accordingly the remnant of the force concentrated in the angle of the " High Wall," an ancient relic of the old wall of Ctesiphon, now a high bank, forming a right angle, each arm being about a quarter of a mile long. During the day the wounded were evacuated, being taken back to Lajj on A. T. carts. It was a pitiable sight seeing these poor fellows go. These were the days before the Mesopotamian Commission—springless carts were all that were available and a number of wounded must have been literally bumped to death over those eight rough miles back to Lajj. The memory of those jolting carts with their grimy battered loads of tortured humanity is one not soon to be forgotten.

The night passed in peace, but the following afternoon the Turks were seen advancing in several columns, and we were given orders to pack up at once. Soon after dark we were ready, but it seemed an age until the head of the column got clear away and our own brigade, who were in rear, could move. Meanwhile the Turks were expected to arrive on the scene at any minute, and everything appeared gloomy in the extreme. Ammunition which could not be removed had been hastily buried. Large fires were lit to help our departure and endeavour to deceive the enemy. Cheerful prospects of rearguard actions all night over unknown country seemed all that was in store for us. However, fortune was with us again ; the Turks hesitated once more and we were not attacked at all during the night. After a weary march through thick dust and sand, we reached Lajj in the early hours of the morning, and were greeted by a heavy downpour, which, fortunately, stopped just before we were quite soaked through.

Digging was again the order as soon as it was light, and arrangements were made to give the Turks a very hot reception if they intended to come on at once.

The following day digging continued, but in the afternoon we were again told to get under way, as the Turks apparently were close upon us.

A long all-night march, only varied by Arab sniping, brought us back to Azizie the following forenoon. Here digging began once more, and it was not at first known if we should remain here and see it out or go back further right down to Kut, some 58 miles. The latter course was decided on next day and, having collected what little of our old kit we could still find, we set off once again southwards, and bivouacked by the river near Umm El Tubul, eleven miles further on.

At eight in the evening, we were just congratulating ourselves on having at last a snug spot for a night's rest, when firing began and our pickets were soon driven in. However, the enemy did not make the expected attack during the night—which we spent in a nullah awaiting him.

As soon as it was light, we could see a large Turkish camp, not much more than a mile distant. The first orders were that we should go out and attack ; so we lined up for this purpose. Just as we were ready, fresh orders arrived, and we retired to the nullah while our guns opened with rapid fire on the Turkish camp. Meanwhile, there was great bustle in our rear, where the transport was being hurriedly got away for a further march towards Kut.

We were told later on that the Turks thought they had only come up against a weak rearguard and were correspondingly dismayed by our gun-fire. They were said to have had 2,000 casualties on this day. However, they pushed on and we had to retire. Previous to this, Turkish shells had been coming over, but not doing very much damage.

The old gun-boat, the *Comet*, and also the *Firefly*, were both put out of action while waiting to cover our retreat, and had to be abandoned to the enemy.

By midday we had shaken off the advancing Turks, having done many miles across country which seemed to grow camel thorn in every direction. This shrub is most unpleasant to march through in shorts, and many were the torn knees in consequence.

A few hours on the ground late that night gave us a little rest ; but it was too cold to sleep, and we were soon sitting up round fires of brushwood which the men had lighted. Many of us had had no food since daybreak, and had to fall back on our emergency rations where these were still in existence.

Next morning we were off once more, and after another long, wearisome day reached a camp only a very few miles from Kut itself, having done over 40 miles in the last 36 hours.

Kut was entered the following morning, December 3rd, but it was not decided till some hours later what position we should take up.

During the next two days we could walk about above ground without molestation, but snipers arrived all too soon, and by Monday, December 6th, Kut was entirely surrounded and the siege had begun.

# CHAPTER II

## KUT

IF the Turks had hurried up, they would have come upon us without properly dug trenches and we should have been taken at a great disadvantage. As it was, however, by the time they did arrive, we were dug in and had a good front line trench, although most of the support and communication trenches still had to be dug. After the first two or three days, all trench work had to be done at night, as conditions by daylight were not healthy.

Life was not particularly pleasant during any part of the siege, and for the first few days we who were outside Kut had no dugouts, all energy being spent on getting the front line firing trench ready. This would have been no hardship but for the fact that we had arrived back in Kut with a biting north wind, causing several degrees of frost at night, and an ice-covered bucket for one's ablutions in the morning.

Throughout the siege, the Tigris formed our only water supply, this being carried in at night in kerosine tins by the regimental bheesties. Drinking water was purified with alum, which got rid of most of the sediment. Tigris is a poor drink at any time and seems particularly nasty when spoiling good whisky.

On Monday, December 6th, the cavalry brigade left at daybreak and were the last people to get away from Kut. Many wounded and sick had been sent down stream during the day or two previously, the lighter cases being left in the hospital at Kut to recover and rejoin.

In those early days, no one thought of a siege lasting more than a month, the general being reputed to be counting on relief by the New Year.

Meanwhile, the Turks had been very busy : not only had they been digging at a furious pace opposite to us and sapping up closer and closer, but they had also sent considerable forces further on down-stream, to near Shaik Saad, to oppose the Relieving Force which was there concentrating.

The night after the cavalry brigade had gone out, the boat bridge over which they had passed to the right bank was demolished under the noses of the enemy.

This gallant feat was performed by Lieut. Matthews, R.E., and Lieut. Sweet, who volunteered for the job. Both men, we hoped, would receive the V.C. By the greatest good fortune, the Turks were entirely surprised, and the bridge was blown up before they realized what was happening or could offer any resistance. Both officers received the D.S.O.

The story of the siege has been told in detail by others, and it is not intended here to attempt it. One saw only one's own small corner, and never knew what to believe of all the rumours and scandal in which a besieged town seems to be particularly prolific.

After the first fortnight, a regular routine was started. The 16th Brigade took alternate turns with the 30th along the main trench line, while the 17th garrisoned the Fort, and the 18th looked after the town itself and Woolpress village.

Meanwhile the medical people had been busy moving from their hospital tents to the covered-in bazaar, which was now converted into wards.

For the first few days, the men were given extra rations to recuperate them after the wearying retreat and for the strenuous trench-digging in progress. It was not until January 10th that we were cut down to two-thirds full rations.

The first Turkish shells arrived on December 5th, but did little harm. Throughout the siege, we had much cause to be thankful for the very large proportion of " duds " amongst all classes of Turkish shell. Fortunately, also, they had no high explosives, or Kut would have been a heap of ruins in no time.

The mud of Mesopotamia deserves mention in this connection. It is as disagreeable as but rather more glutinous than most other brands of the same substance, and when baked dry by the sun is singularly impenetrable to rifle bullets. All the rules found in military pocket-books were quite upset by it, some eight inches of the best variety being quite enough to stop any bullet. For the same reason, trench digging in some places was very slow and tedious work, as the ground at that time was dry and hard, seeming more like cast iron than anything else.

During the early part of the siege, regiments in the 16th and 30th Brigades, on being relieved in the front line, returned to a bivouac in Kut and did some hours' digging on the way, the operation being carried out

at night. The following night was as a rule
allowed us in peace, but for the next three or
six nights, until again relieved, one was
generally out digging or in " support " to
some part of the line, so that " being relieved " did not mean much rest for anybody.
The bivouac had a further disadvantage
in that we had as many casualties here as in
the front line. Dropping bullets would come
in at odd moments from all directions, and
it was impossible to keep clear of them.
Some unfortunate was laid out nearly every
day in this way.

The Turks never once tried to shell our
front line, but spent all their attentions on
the town and the Fort. A tremendous
" hate " preceded their attack on the latter
on Christmas Eve. They succeeded in blow-
ing a breach in the mud wall of the Fort in
the north-east bastion, and afterwards as-
saulted with great dash. Fighting was ex-
tremely fierce and the Turks lost very heavily
from our machine-guns. There was much
hand bombing, this being the only occasion
during the siege when fighting at close
quarters took place.

After gaining a footing through the breach
into our trenches, the Turks were dislodged,
but came on again later, and at midnight,

December 24th, were still in possession of the north-east bastion. However, they thought better of it, and by the morning of December 25th had all disappeared again. As a result of this fighting, we had about 400 casualties, while the Turks were said to have lost 2,000. Be that as it may, they never made another attack on our lines.

Khalil Pasha, the Turkish commander, was said afterwards to have told one of the British generals that he was just preparing another tremendous attack at the end of January, meaning to smash his way into Kut at any cost, when the floods intervened, and drove him back over half a mile, while we had also to return to the " middle " line—our second line trench some 300 yards behind the first. He stated that he was prepared to lose 10,000 in the attempt.

Christmas Day passed peacefully, much to our satisfaction, and from now onwards there was great speculation as to the day of relief. We knew that General Aylmer's force was to start during the first days of January, and it was predicted that by January 9th or 10th the siege would be over.

By the first week in January, all fresh meat was finished, but for a time we had " bully."

The Relieving Force suffered its first serious check at Shaik Saad and never arrived, as we had hoped. There was nothing to be done but to carry on and wait till next time. The weather now was cold and wet and the trenches often knee deep in mud and water. Kut itself was in a filthy state, the streets being a sea of mud after every downpour. The Tigris was steadily rising throughout January and by the 20th was near the top of the bund running along the bank. Heavy rain on this day and the next, together with the rise in the river, was responsible for flooding out the Turks' front line They managed, however, to turn the water over towards us, with the result that we, also, were drowned out of the corresponding part of our line, the effect of this being that there was now a good distance between the new front lines. For two days we could walk about in the open, and were much interested in seeing the old Turkish trenches, and taking all possible firewood in the shape of old ammunition boxes from their loopholes. We found that one of their saps was only forty yards from our trench, and many were the bombs they had thrown which just fell short.

The most interesting relics were numbers

of pamphlets tied to sticks and bits of earth and thrown towards our line. These were effusions printed in various languages by the Indian National Society, Chicago,[1] and contained much startling information. The Sepoys were informed that no British were now left in several N.W. Frontier districts, and were recommended, as brave soldiers, to murder their British officers and join the Turks. The Sultan was represented as being ready to give land to every one who would respond to this invitation. As regards Gallipoli, it was stated that Sir Ian Hamilton had been wounded and that Lord Kitchener had run away in the night, taking the British troops with him and leaving the Indians, who thereupon murdered their officers and joined the Turks.

Very few, if any, of these leaflets reached the Sepoys, and, as far as we could see, left them unmoved.

After two days' freedom above ground, a reconnaissance was sent out to locate the Turkish outposts. This had the immediate effect of starting great activity in the Turkish pickets some 1,200 yards from our line, and from that day onwards snipers were always

---

[1] See Appendix B.

busy. Even so, life was very much pleasanter than when the enemy was within 100 yards.

By January 13th we were down to half rations, and by January 23rd were still further reduced. On the 26th, the general issued a long *communiqué*, telling us of how the Relieving Force had been unsuccessful so far, having had heavy losses and very bad weather to contend against. He announced that there were 84 days' more ample rations without counting the 3,000 animals.

Actually the siege went on for another 94 days, but the rations were scarcely ample, even including the horse meat. However, at the time, it seemed that there was nothing to worry about, especially as the general said he was confident of being relieved during the first half of February.

With the beginning of February, we started eating horse, mule and camel. There were very few camels, but they were said to be quite good eating. For the rest, mule is very much to be preferred to horse. There were also the heavy battery bullocks, but these were not numerous, and were very thin already.

All the eggs and milk obtainable from Arabs in the town were supposed to go to the hospitals, but it was always said they did not receive nearly as much as they should have done.

During January and February, one could buy several things from Arabs in the bazaar, i.e., tea, dried beans, atta and "kabobs" or small hot chapatties, cooked in grease. The tea must all originally have come from the S. & T. All the Arabs in Kut wore Army socks very early in the siege. In fact, it would be harder to find a race of more expert thieves anywhere on the globe.

Towards the middle of February, the Turks began sending over an aeroplane to bomb us. The pilot was a German, and knew his business too well. After his first trip, machine guns were rigged up to welcome him the next time he came and the sappers mounted a 13-pounder to fire as an anti-aircraft gun.

Considering the difficulties involved and the absence of all special sighting arrangements this gun made some very fair shooting. But the only effect of all these efforts was to make Fritz, the pilot, fly higher and approach the town from a different direction. The first time he came very little damage was done ; then one day a bomb demolished an Arab house, killing a number of women and children, and a second fell on the British hospital, where no less than 32 sick and wounded men were killed outright or horribly injured. The padre—the Rev. H. Spooner—told me afterwards that no sight he had witnessed at Ctesiphon could be compared to that hospital ward. Presumably Fritz was aiming at the ordnance yard next door or some of the guns on the river bank only a little further on. Had there been more room and good buildings in Kut, it would no doubt have been possible to put the hospital in a safer spot, but, as it was, no other building was available. Fritz always succeeded in eluding our aeroplanes from the Relieving Force. He had so little distance to go home, whereas they had to come up 20 miles or more.

Two main observation posts were maintained, one above general headquarters in the town, and the other in the Fort. There was great rivalry between the two, and on one occasion, a large flock of sheep was definitely reported in the town as a considerable force of the enemy moving to the rear. The Fort maintained they were sheep and neither would give in.

We could see every day long strings of camels on the horizon, carrying rations for the Turks from their base at Shamrán above

Kut down to their forces at Sanaiyat and Magassis.

The usual book of words about camels informs the reader that they are liable to slip and split themselves up if allowed to travel over wet or slippery ground. In Mesopotamia, however, the camel seems not to worry at all when going over land submerged by floods, and carrying on generally under all conditions. He is a much wilder specimen than the usual Indian camel, and our experience before Ctesiphon was that he would only lie down if one of his forelegs was folded and bound up, and he was then hit on the head with a thick stick.

A feature of Kut which will not be forgotten was the little chapel which our padre rigged up in one of the few remaining upper rooms of the battered Serai. This building was in an exposed position on the river bank and suffered more than any other from the Turkish shells. The padre himself was indefatigable, doing everything he possibly could in the hospitals in addition to his other duties.

Almost every day one or more of our aeroplanes came over Kut, and some things were dropped, but how we wished they would drop us some letters. We knew there must be a great accumulation of mails at Amara and it seemed so easy to arrange it. As it was, some bags of letters were dropped for the staff and even the S. & T. but, as usual, the regimental officers came off worst. We wanted news from home more than anything else, and, as it turned out, most of us never heard a word from our people till we had reached Anatolia the following July after an interval of eight months.

Fortunately, we could get messages sent out by the wireless, and once a month a telegram was despatched to the depots in India, saying that all were well, or something equally brief but satisfactory to our friends at home.

Another great blessing afforded by the wireless was the publication of a short summary of Reuter's telegrams, which gave us something else to talk of other than the everlasting questions of food and the date of relief. In particular, the taking of Erzerum by the Russians cheered us up, and made us hope that the Russian force approaching Bagdad from Persia would be equally successful.

In fact, at one time the betting was said to be in favour of the Russian general, Baratoff, relieving us from the north, before our friends down-stream.

With the arrival of March, every one was full of excitement over the coming great effort of the relieving force, which was prophesied to take place on the 4th, but was actually the 8th.

Many schemes were prepared by which we were to co-operate, so that after the Turks had been started off rearwards by General Aylmer, we might hasten their departure. In most of these plans one brigade would have to play the leading rôle, and probably come in for a pretty hot time unless the Turks had become quite demoralised ; much speculation arose, therefore, as to which brigade would be given this post of honour.

March 8th came and went and we realized that another gallant attempt had failed. The bombardment could be clearly heard, and at night it was easy to see the shells bursting. During the attack on the Dujailah Redoubt our friends were only seven to eight miles from us, and we could hear their rifle and machine gun-fire.

This failure was a great disappointment and we realized what it must have cost in casualties. There was only one thing for us to do, namely, carry on ; so the rations were reduced again and life went on in its, by this time, mechanical round. All were still confident of being relieved, and when it became known that General Gorringe had taken over command down stream we felt sure something decisive would happen and that he would get through, if anyone could.

After every unsuccessful attempt, a Turkish envoy promptly arrived with a white flag and requested us politely to surrender. He was as courteously and consistently refused.

Rations were now down to 10 oz. of bread, this being half atta and half barley. The dates were finished and the small stocks of mess stores which had been carefully eked out were nearly finished. Still we had jam and tea and the mule wasn't at all bad. Some saccharine dropped by aeroplane gave us something sweet, and was a great blessing.

The efforts to get the Indians to eat meat at the end of February had failed. They declared that every village pundit would be against them on their return to India and that, in consequence, no one would give them their daughters to marry.

Everything possible to help religious scruples was done, and special permission obtained from the Imám at Delhi and other religious authorities ; but it was no use, and not until the second week in April, when they were literally starving, did the Indian troops begin eating horse. No doubt, if they had done so earlier, we could have held out for some few days longer, but it is doubtful whether this would have sufficed for our relief.

After March 8th, all horses not wanted for food were shot to save their keep, and many a good animal was sacrificed in this way.

By the 19th, the bread ration was only ½ lb., while the Indians were getting 10 oz. meal. The small quantity of food began now to tell on the strength of all ranks, and cases of bad enteritis—so-called—were common, these resulting in many deaths during the last days of the siege.

It is really wonderful what an amount of satisfaction can be derived, under such conditions, from simply imagining a first-class meal, and I remember one day, in my dug-out, having a great time going through a long menu and choosing everything I should like best.

When the grass began to grow towards the end of March, we gathered what the Sepoys called ság or anything we could make a sort of spinach with. It was like eating wet hay, but, undoubtedly, kept scurvy down, and if well soaked in vinegar was not so bad.

In Woolpress they managed to get a little fish from the river, fishing by night.

Our activities after March 8th were directed to keeping out the floods. Two big bunds were made, one inside the other, round Kut. The Arabs in the town were forced to work on the inner one and thus saved the troops, who were weak enough as it was already with making the outer bund.

By the end of March we had a splendid bund across the middle line capable of keeping out nearly three feet of water ; this being 4 ft. 6 in. high and about 20 ft. thick at the base, all the soil having to be excavated from pits in front. The sappers had told us that our mess dug-out was just about the lowest spot round Kut and would be the first place to be flooded ; however, when the floods really came, we found we were two feet higher up than the regiment a little further along the line. It was hard work making these bunds, and all the men not otherwise on duty were out every night. The bund also had to form the firing parapet, and with barbed wire entanglements in the " borrow " pits in front and again beyond we were well protected from any attack, not to mention the floods which would have made an advance by the enemy almost impossible.

All through April the water slowly percolated up and the dug-outs and trenches had to be continually raised, until by the end of the month we were nearly up to ground level. The river rose to its highest level during April, but fortunately news was received, by wireless, from a British officer with the Russians at Lake Urmia, of the various floods, so that we were more or less prepared. Actually we had never much more than 2 ft. 6 in. outside our bund, which held well. Had we been driven back inside the inner bund, the whole force would have been cooped up in a very small area and any shelling would have been bound to take a large toll.

For the last ten days there was no tobacco left. People were smoking used-up tea-leaves, orange leaves, liquorice, and even grass. Whatever smoking tea-leaves may be like for the smoker, it is exceedingly unpleasant for everybody else, especially in a dug-out.

Throughout the April fighting we followed each *communiqué* from General Gorringe with the greatest anxiety, watching his shells bursting over the Turkish lines by night and always hoping on until after the *Julnar* had failed to get through.

The men were not told anything about this attempt, but the 30th Brigade made ready to cover the unloading, in the event of the gallant ship winning through. She was to be beached by the Fort the same night and unloaded before the Turks could bring their guns to bear on her next morning. I remember listening to the firing as she slowly made her way up-stream ; star-shells and flares went up and lit up the scene and she met with a terrible reception.

Then, after a time, all firing ceased and we realized that this splendid attempt had failed. According to one member of the crew, all went well until they reached Magassis, where they struck a cable which gave way, but a second one immediately afterwards stopped them. Commander Firman, the naval officer in charge, thought this was a sand-bank and left his protection on the bridge to shout to them to take a sounding. He was killed on the spot. Cowley, the well-known skipper of the ship, then took charge but they could not get past the obstruction, and he himself was soon very severely wounded by a shell, from which he died when taken ashore.

Eventually this magnificent attempt had to be given up. It was a most heroic effort and, had it been possible to steam faster, would probably have been successful. As it was, the ship was very heavily laden with a month's supplies for the garrison on board and could only do five or six knots against the very strong current. Even so, we still fondly hoped that General Gorringe might achieve the impossible at the last minute ; but it was not to be.

The last few days we lived on the emergency and reserve rations which each regiment had in its keeping, and the food dropped by aeroplanes from the Relieving Force. These brought us white flour, some sugar and a little chocolate. The bread ration, however, was only 4 oz. or just one good slice a day each.

We were all very weak and there was a great deal of sickness. Enteritis, which seemed not very different from cholera, was prevalent and affected nearly everybody to some extent. Not infrequently a Tommy going into Kut from the front line would suddenly collapse, often not to recover. I remember feeling rather disappointed that I did not look thinner, and one felt one ought to be a dreadful scarecrow really to have done the siege justice.

D

# CHAPTER III

ON April 29th, Kut surrendered, and it was with sad feelings that we watched two Turkish battalions marching in at midday. The bitter thought that they should have worsted us in the end, together with the knowledge of the useless sacrifice of life by our friends down-stream, was present to all; but there was also a great feeling of relief that the siege was now over, and we had not realized until this moment how severe the strain had been.

We believed the Turks would treat all ranks well, as up to that moment they had always fought and behaved like gentlemen. Khalil Pasha, the Turkish general, had said we should be treated as his "honoured guests," and, since at that time we had not had much experience of Turkish promises, we were inclined to think all would be well, although we knew the Turks themselves were short of supplies and had great difficulty in feeding their troops downstream.

Orders came round telling us to destroy everything that could be of use to the enemy, only a few rifles being kept in case of trouble with Arabs in the town before the Turks arrived. Field-glasses, revolvers, maps, and diaries all had to be destroyed and saddlery burnt. It seemed a crime to be sacrificing so much that was valuable, but this was better than helping the enemy in any way. The last works of destruction had only just been completed when the Turkish troops arrived, and great was their disgust at finding all the guns destroyed, and nothing worth taking but a few rifles.

Some of us had kept our swords, thinking that they would be returned to us in traditional style, only to find them collected by the first Turkish subaltern or N.C.O. who set eyes on them. Those who were wiser had thrown theirs in the river or buried them, and we all wished we had done the same. Later on, we heard that the officers' swords from Kut had been displayed as an interesting exhibit in some museum at Constantinople.

The departure from Kut began that evening, one steamer taking a full load up to Shamrán, the Turkish base camp, some eight miles up-stream. We had still to depend on the remnants of our own rations for that day and the next, but fortunately they just sufficed.

Next day, as we moved up towards the old Serai, near which the steamers were moored, we had to pass a palm grove which had been occupied by some Turkish soldiers. These men were systematically looting any kit which was being carried past, and to which they had taken a fancy. A good deal was lost in this way. The Turkish officers seemed powerless to stop it, the culprits merely walking away until the officer had departed.

The steamer made two or three more trips that day, but it was announced at noon that all those left must march, their kit alone going on the steamer. How they managed that march in a starving condition they only know who did it, but when the steamer reached Shamrán on its last trip at midnight they had all come in and been regaled with Turkish ration biscuits. An amusing incident occurred during this march. An Indian sweeper—the humblest of all regimental followers—was trudging along behind his regiment carrying some of the articles of his trade, when they passed some Turkish gunpits where there were several German officers standing. On seeing them the sweeper made obeisance with the deepest of salaams ; whereupon the Germans promptly stood to attention, clicked their heels and saluted.

During the following days, we made ourselves as comfortable as possible at Shamrán, and, fortunately, got other food in addition to the Turkish biscuits. These biscuits need only be once seen or eaten never to be forgotten. They are of a dark-brown colour, unless mouldy, about six inches in diameter and an inch thick in the centre, and made from a very coarse meal, which must contain anything except wheat. They are even harder than the hardest of our own army biscuits.

The Turks had allowed us to bring with us what tents we had in Kut, and, although we had to leave them behind at Shamrán, they were of the greatest comfort to us during the week which we spent there.

A launch arrived from the relieving force, bringing with it barges laden with food, including a number of mess stores and gifts. These we eventually got possession of, although the Turks would not allow them to be landed at our camp, but took them up-stream some distance, where we expected they would take a systematic toll of everything. Turkish soldiers and Arabs brought in dates, a few oranges, and a syrup made from dates, which they sold at excessive prices.

Bathing was allowed in the river, and some enthusiasts who still had fishing tackle spent a considerable time on the bank, but without much success.

One day, General Townshend passed upstream in a launch accompanied by two or three of his staff *en route* to Bagdad. All ranks rushed to the bank to give him a parting cheer, which one felt meant that all knew he had done his best for us throughout.

With the end of the siege one had expected all the worst features of the last few weeks to disappear, but the heavy mortality from enteritis continued at Shamrán. It was especially heavy amongst the British ranks, in many cases being aggravated by a too suddenly increased diet, of which the Turkish biscuits formed a large part.

A few days after our arrival, it was announced that the men would all have to march up, while officers would be taken up in batches by the steamers. The first party to leave contained the generals and staff, and most of the officers from British units. The following day the men were to march. Our doctors insisted on a very thorough examination, as a large proportion of the men were unable to march. The Turks would not, however, accept the British doctors' decisions, and reduced the unfit to a much smaller number.

The result was that large numbers fell out after the first day, and had to be taken on board the *Julnar*, which was bringing up a number of men from the Kut hospitals whom the Turks considered not ill enough to be exchanged. We were all convinced that had it not been for German counsels at Constantinople some arrangement for our return on *parole* to India might have been made.

The men were told to take one blanket or greatcoat each, as well as their haversacks and water-bottles. They had no transport whatever, and our hearts misgave us as we watched them go. The column wound slowly out of the camp with many checks, and it was over an hour before they were clear ; all seemed to be carrying big loads, and many things must have been thrown away or sold before they reached Bagdad. The Turks were only too anxious to buy, when they could not steal any clothing, boots, or equipment, their own clothing and equipment being at a very low ebb after months of service in Mesopotamia, to say nothing of the long march down from Asia Minor.

Many had no boots, and were just wearing sandals of goat-skin, such as they are accustomed to use in the country districts of Anatolia.

When the men had departed, the camp seemed very forlorn ; about 150 British and Indian officers were left, while the hospital tents contained many sick of all ranks.

Two days later, on May 10th, the second party of officers left on the steamer *Khalifa*, which had on board a few German gunners returning to Bagdad and a good number of Turkish officers. The journey took three days ; on the second day we passed the *Julnar*. She was covered with bullet-marks, showing through what a severe fire she had forced her way. Now she was loaded with sick from Kut. We waved to those on board, but were not near enough to speak to them.

Our steamer used to tie up to the bank for a short while twice a day, in the morning and evening, enabling us to get a hurried bathe and a little change from the cramped space on the deck, where we spent the rest of the time.

The third day we passed the battlefield of Ctesiphon, full of memories of the victory which had proved so disastrous six months before. We halted for the night not far from the Arch, and were greeted by the local Arabs, who danced and fired off ancient rifles and pistols in the air in derision at our captivity. The women also contributed their share by making a peculiar kind of trilling sound. How we hoped they might soon be singing in a very different fashion when our troops should advance again and take Bagdad.

We reached Bagdad the next morning. As we slowly paddled up the river, we could see the Red Crescent flag floating from almost every good house on the river sides ; hospitals seemed to be everywhere, and we realized what awful casualties the Relieving Force had inflicted on the Turks.

For some miles before Bagdad is reached, the river is fringed with palm groves, gardens, and cultivated land. When we left Kut the river was within a few feet of the highest ground, but here the banks were very much higher.

We were landed at the old British Residency, and, after a little delay, were formed up in order of seniority and marched off along what appeared to be the main road. It was evidently arranged as a triumphal procession to impress the inhabitants. At length, after a march of two miles, passing through the covered-in bazaar, where the shade was most welcome, we emerged on the north side of the town, and reached our destination at the Cavalry Barracks. We had been promised furnished quarters, but found bare floors and empty rooms ; the building formed a large quadrangle, and was empty of all troops when we arrived. A little later our orderlies and servants appeared, bringing our kit from the steamer. On leaving Shamrán colonels were allowed to take two order- lies or Indian servants, other officers being allowed one each.

Fortunately, just before we left, some money in Turkish gold had been sent up by the Relieving Force by aeroplane, and thus all ranks had a little cash.

When the second party reached Bagdad, the first party had already departed for Mosul, and rumours arose about the journey, people saying at first that we should have carriages from the railhead at Samarra, then that only donkeys would be available, while others thought we should be lucky to get anything.

While at the barracks we were given a month's pay by the Turkish authorities, on what proved to be for senior officers a very generous scale, the greatest mercy being that half the amount was paid in gold. Had this not been done, we should have been in a truly sorry plight on the long journeys by road across the desert, since no Arab would look at Turkish notes, and insisted on being paid in hard cash.

At this time, the Russian force under General Baratoff had made a sudden advance through the Pusht-i-Kuh mountains and reached Khanikin, 90 miles north-east of Bagdad; the Turks were therefore very anxious to get us away, while some of the under-strappers, evidently thinking the Russians would reach Bagdad, began to talk in a very different strain, pretending that they had really been pro-British all the time.

Very few people succeeded in getting out of the barracks, but two or three officers, duly escorted, managed to get a gharry, and drove straight to the American consul, who arranged to give them money, and did everything he could for them. He said he expected to see many of us, and went on to tell them exactly what he thought of the campaign up to date. He was very pessimistic over the future treatment of the British troops, and declared that had we known what would happen to them we would have cut our way out of Kut at whatever cost. We hoped this was exaggeration, and that things would not turn out as badly as he expected ; but events proved only too truly how entirely his fears were justified. Hopelessly inadequate rations, no transport, no medical arrangements for the sick who fell out, and utter incapability of all Turkish authorities, constitute one of the blackest crimes committed during any war.

It is only right to add that whenever we met German officers they did all they could to help us, more than one saying they considered that we and they were civilized people in a land of barbarians.

Two days after reaching Bagdad we were paraded in the hot sun in the afternoon and marched off to the station, passing over the bridge of boats and through the Shia quarter of the city, which lies on the right bank of the river. We were all only too glad to get away from the insanitary conditions which are inseparable from all Turkish buildings.

After a wait of two hours at the station, we were packed into a train which started about six o'clock. A few miles north of Bagdad we passed the Great Mosque at Kazmain, its golden domes and minarets shining in the setting sun. The train proceeded at a good rate ; everything in connection with the railway was naturally German, and of a substantial description. The length of line then completed to the railhead at Samaria was 80 miles, passing through slightly undulating country the whole way. This had been finished by the Germans before the war broke out.

Most of us were weary, and many preferred lying on the floor of the corridors or vestibules at the end of the cars, to sitting straight up in the cramped compartments. We made several halts, and it was near midnight when we arrived. Our guards, a few gendarmes, seemed to have no idea where we were going, or what was to be done with us. Eventually we were told to leave our kit, which was to be brought along later, and were guided down towards the river. After walking a mile, we found ourselves in a small Arab village on the river bank, and were conducted into a courtyard some 40 yards square, where we were told we were to stay. There was a rough shelter round three sides, formed by brush-wood supported on a rough wooden framework; this promised a certain amount of shade, and we were all glad to be in the open air rather than in another barrack building. There were no signs of any transport fetching our kit, so the most enterprising managed to procure two trollies, and trundled them up

to the station along a narrow-gauge line.
The Turks used this line for taking stores,
ammunition, etc., to the railway, from the
rafts on which they were floated down from
Mosul. By dawn, nearly all the kit had been
collected, and we had settled down as best
we could.

There was a certain amount of food obtainable from Arab vendors, and as we had our
Indian servants, and a few things left from
stores received at Shamrán, we were fairly
comfortable. As usual, no one seemed to
know how long we were to be there, before our
journey by road across the desert began.
Fortunately, we were not guarded very
strictly, and were allowed to go outside the
courtyard, and down to the river to bathe;
the current here was very strong, and only
the most powerful swimmers could make any
headway against it, and that only for a few
yards.

The town of Samarra was on the other
bank, and some little height above the land
on our side. It stands back from the river,
and contains a fine mosque, with a golden
dome. The inhabitants cross the river in
gufahs—the large round coracles which are
used all down the Tigris. Owing to the
current a start always has to be made very

much higher up-stream than the point where it is desired to land on the other side.

During the three or four days which we spent at Samarra, a large quantity of German gun-ammunition arrived by raft from up-stream, and was carried by Arabs up the bank to the trollies. These rafts carry big loads; they are formed by a skeleton frame of wood on which is placed brushwood, the frame being supported by inflated skins which are tied to it. On reaching the end of a journey, the skins are deflated and sent back up the river to be used again. As there are rapids between Samarra and Bagdad, it was not possible to float the rafts right down to Bagdad, and consequently every-thing had to be transhipped to the railway. One night some large motors arrived, and went on at once by road towards Bagdad. Reports immediately circulated that Enver Pasha had arrived; but this cannot have been true.

We had now learnt who our commandant on the journey was to be. He was a yuz-bashi or captain, by name Elmey Bey, a little man with an enormous moustache, which made him look very fierce. He knew a very little French, and could therefore be approached without an interpreter. We did not really appreciate him until later. One morning he escorted a few of us over to the town ; there was nothing to be seen except the mosque, and we were not allowed to look at this even from the gateway, much less to enter the courtyard.

After making a few purchases, we went into an Arab café and partook of coffee and tea flavoured with citron. Elmey Bey would not let us pay for anything, and we thought it most hospitable of him. He said he would accept our hospitality another day. However, he eventually left the café without paying anything, and apparently the proprietor was really our unwilling host.

The town seemed very deserted, many of the inhabitants being over on the other side, selling anything they could to the first batch of troops, who had reached Samarra that morning by rail, and were now camped in the open a little way above us. We were not allowed to go to see them, but one or two managed to get messages through, and an Indian clerk belonging to my regiment came to see us. He looked thin, and had evidently had a hard time. He said that on the way to Bagdad the guards had flogged men who fell out, to see if they were really ill, and that conditions as regards rations were pretty

ELMEY BEY
(*From a Watercolour Drawing by Lt. Browne*)

bad generally. None of our men, however, had succumbed so far, and, as many of the regiment had been anything but fit to start with, we hoped they would be able to stand it. We gave him a few little things in the way of eatables before he went back.

The next day, we were told we were going to march ; and the question of transport became all-important. At first the Turks said there would be two animals—donkeys, mules, or ponies—to each officer ; this seemed much too good to be true, and when the time came there was barely one animal to every officer. These had all been forcibly commandeered from the villagers round, and a good many were taken back again on the sly by their owners before we could get hold of them. Others were taken by the gendarmes who formed our guard, while several were too small to be of use, or were hopelessly lame. By the time we had got our kit packed, we had left for riding one reasonably large donkey and a diminutive beast between the six officers and seven Indian servants in our mess.

We started at sunset in a dust-storm. Fortunately it did not last long, and we got along without mishap till about eleven o'clock, when a heavy rainstorm came on. All through

E

the night, and especially after every halt, we had been urged on by our Arab escort shouting " Yallah, yallah ! " This really means " O God ! " but is used by the Arabs for " Get on and hurry up." How we came to loathe that cry ! About two in the morning, we reached some water ; luckily, in the dark, we could not see what we were drinking. We must have done fifteen to twenty miles ; and, as most of us had not marched any distance for months, we were only too glad to fall asleep for a few hours. At dawn we were again on the move, having had some trouble in finding our own animals again ; the wise had marked theirs with copying pencil, and this method was generally resorted to afterwards.

We went on with halts of a few minutes every hour, and got down to the river again at midday. It was now pretty hot, and we were told we should arrive at Tekrit, a small Arab town, in one hour. Throughout Turkey and Mesopotamia distances are measured by hours ; a good working plan is to add on 50 per cent. to the average of what one is told, as no two men will ever say the same ; if journeying by night it is safer to double it.

That last hour to Tekrit was one of the worst we had ; actually it was nearer two hours.

There was a blazing sun, and we were very tired. The road left the river and went up a hill, then down and up again. On each rise we expected to see the town, but it was dreadfully slow in appearing. From some distance off we were met by Arab boys and women selling eggs, raisins, sour curds, and chapatties. Finally, we were taken through the place down to the river edge, a sort of dirty, stony beach, where we were told to camp ; we had covered 30 to 35 miles in the last nineteen hours, and most of us had marched almost the whole distance.

There was a small Arab café which we were allowed to use, but otherwise there was no shade. Arabs sauntered about our bivouac, and were anything but friendly ; the place was filthy, and we were far from feeling cheerful.

Some of the houses of the town stand up on a rocky crag above the river. Tekrit is a very old place, and at one time there was a bridge over the river here. It was laid waste by the Mongols and the people butchered. Before we left, we were all wishing that some such fate might be in store for the present inhabitants.

Some of us bathed, but the water was very shallow and dirty. Arabs could be seen swimming across the river supported on inflated skins, in exactly the same way as Xenophon has described their forefathers doing 2,000 years ago.

That afternoon we tried to arrange to hire extra animals, as we felt that we could never get along if the succeeding marches were so severe. A good many animals were forthcoming, mostly mules and large donkeys. The usual terms were to be one pound in gold, paid in advance, and a second on arrival at Mosul. The following evening, just before starting, the owners demanded the whole two pounds in advance ; there was nothing for it but to comply, the reason undoubtedly being that the commandant of the town and Elmey Bey both desired to have their share before starting, as otherwise they would not see any of it. A long delay ensued before we got off, and it was getting dark before we were clear of the town.

The march that night was uneventful, and we halted for a few hours before dawn near the river, continuing our way as soon as it got light. We passed a few Arab encampments, formed of dark tents, where the nomads come at certain seasons to cultivate the surrounding land, together with their flocks of sheep and goats. Not a single house, or even mud-hut, was to be seen. Our next halt, which we reached in the middle of the morning, was a serai standing by itself on a low ridge. It was built on the usual square pattern, and contained a well, which however, was not of very much use, as the water was unfit for drinking ; drinking water had all to be carried from the river, over a mile away.

Elmey Bey, or " Phil May," as we christened him, had by this time shown how anxious he was to help us, by doing nothing at all to assist us either in buying provisions or keeping prices down. Our escort consisted of a few Arab gendarmes, and, on arrival at any village or encampment, they would make the people put up their prices, and insist on taking the difference as commission themselves ; whenever they could manage it they prevented all country people from approaching us until their own demands had been satisfied.

Phil May rode the whole way, and would hurry on and be comfortably asleep in his camp bed by the time we reached the end of the march. If worried sufficiently by the senior officers, he would occasionally go to the extent of abusing one or more of the gendarmes, and administer the usual

punishment adopted by all officers in the
Turkish army—slapping the face of the culprit.
It says a good deal for the discipline of the
Turkish soldier that a sergeant will stand up
like a lamb and have his face smacked by
the veriest nincompoop of an officer.

Leaving the serai again the following morning, we did a short march of some six or
seven miles only, down to the river. This
was to be a very strenuous day, for that
evening we were to start on the long waterless march about which we had heard so
much. It was said to be 40 miles, that we
should halt during the next day, and not
reach water till the morning after, thus doing
two all-night marches. Most people had
bought goatskins, tied up to hold water, from
the local Arabs. Most of them leaked more or
less rapidly, the new skins being much the worst,
and all gave the water a very strong flavour.

We got away about 5 p.m., and nothing
special happened till about 11 o'clock, when
suddenly the escort became wildly excited,
and dashed up and down ; we were halted
and told there were hostile Arabs about ;
the gendarmes fired off a few shots into the
air, but nothing more occurred. All we
could find to account for the disturbance
was that one officer had lost his donkey,

which had got loose and gone careering off to the side of the road. As it was a dark night, this may very likely have alarmed one or two of the gendarmes, who did not strike us as being men of valour.

Two hours later we halted, and, after a sketchy supper, soon got to sleep. In the morning, instead of remaining where we were for the day, as we had expected, we had to move on once more to the tune of " Yallah, yallah." After three hours or so we reached some low sand-hills, and amongst these found an unexpected stream, where we proceeded to camp. This stream, like so many more in this part of the world, was not pure water, but contained salts of various descriptions, said by the Turks to make the water bad for drinking. We drank steadily from this and other similar streams ; and, luckily, for the most part, felt no ill effects.

That evening, we were again upon the road, our destination being Shilgat, a small Turkish post on the Tigris, which we were meeting once more. We arrived eventually about midnight, after a very wearisome march, and after a long wait were herded into the courtyard of the Turkish fort. When the kit had been sorted out, we were very soon asleep, the usual precautions being taken to see that boots were hidden under one's valise, or tied up in some way to prevent theft. As the Turkish troops were always badly off for footgear, boots were the articles most often stolen, and several pairs had disappeared in this way before we reached our journey's end. All were thoroughly tired out, and it had been decided that we would insist on a rest the following day. Great was our wrath, therefore, to find ourselves awakened again at dawn, and told we must move at once to another place. Phil May came in for more abuse, and lost his temper promptly. We settled down, eventually, in another enclosure not far away, where we had more room. Later on, we succeeded in our efforts to get a whole day's rest.

In ancient times Shilgat was Assur, the first capital of the Assyrian Empire. Archæologists had evidently been at work here; all the foundations of the old city had been laid bare; it had covered a considerable area, and had been built largely of marble. Situated on a high promontory overlooking the Tigris and the flat plains beyond, the old town must have been an imposing sight from all the surrounding country. Now, only the foundations remain, and no carving or inscriptions are to be seen.

Next day, we were off once more across flat, uninteresting country, keeping close to the river. At the start, there was considerable delay owing to donkeys getting bogged in a creek which we had to cross. After a midday halt for a couple of hours, we continued our weary way, and finally bivouacked for the night on the bank of the river.

The following day's march proved one of the most unpleasant of the whole journey. After an early start, we soon reached a Turkish post, where a long delay occurred while our orderlies drew rations. At this place there were small bitumen works, these being the first signs of any modern industry which we had seen since leaving Bagdad. A little farther on, the track rose to higher ground, and we left the river away on our right. It began to get hot towards midday, and a warm wind got up, bringing clouds of dust to meet us. At length, in the afternoon, we reached a Turkish post, where after much altercation we were refused an entrance, and had to retrace our steps to a somewhat sulphurous stream a little way back, where we camped for the night.

The country all round at this time of year is covered with long thin grass, and in many places there are quantities of wild flowers, scarlet poppies being very conspicuous.

In order to defeat the gendarmes, we had by now formed a kind of trade union for buying eggs from villagers. On approaching each place, it was decided how much should be paid for eggs, these being more in demand than any other kind of food. In the Bagdad district the Persian kron is the usual unit : a kron is equivalent to fourpence or two Turkish piastres ; farther north the piastre, or qrush, is used. The cheapest rate we obtained for eggs was eight for a piastre, or four a penny, whereas when the gendarmes had their own way we had to pay a penny for each.

Our next march took us to Hamàmali, a place on the river, and containing an old bath, as its name implies. There are bitumen springs entering the river here, but they are not strong enough to render the water unfit for drinking. Supplies were very plentiful—eggs, raisins, bread, and dates being the most sought after. After a few hours' rest and a bathe in the river, we started off again in the evening, looking forward to a real rest on reaching Mosul the next day. We bivouacked beside the road, and were moving at an early hour next morning. The road wound

up and down over low hills, and some attempt
had been made to metal the surface and build
good bridges, showing that we were getting
near to an important place.   As we reached
the top of one ridge, a full view of the Tigris
valley burst upon us, Mosul lying straight
ahead of us, while farther to the right across
the river lay the ruins of old Nineveh.   In the
immediate foreground, the course of the river
was marked by green cultivated land and
low woods, while away, in the distance, rose
the dark mountains of Kurdistan.

On approaching the town more closely,
one noticed a great difference in the mosques,
as compared with Bagdad.   Here the minarets were of plain stone-work, and were not
capped by gorgeous golden domes or brilliant
blue tile-work.

We were marched into a large building,
formed on the usual Turkish pattern of a
hollow square.   This seemed to be chiefly
used as a prison.   We were given three or four
empty rooms on the upper story.   Water
was scarce, and had to be brought in by hand.
In other respects, the building had all the filthy
characteristics inseparable from the Turk.

Soon after arriving, we were given Red
Crescent post-cards to send home, and these
turned out to be the first news  our friends

in England received from us.  For food we
were allowed to go out to restaurants in the
town.  One of these, run by a Frenchman,
was a great joy to us, after the scratch meals
which we had been forced to be content
with for so long.  We had covered the 175
miles from Samarra to Mosul in just under
ten days, and had it not been for the extra
animals hired at Tekrit we should scarcely
have managed this.  As it was, most people
could ride for an hour and walk for an
hour alternately, though some were not so
fortunate.

We were promised many things in Mosul,
amongst others that we should be allowed to
go to bathe in the river.  This was never
allowed in the end, although we went in parties
to the bazaar, where we laid in stocks of
flour, rice, and raisins, for the journey on
to Ras-el-Ain.  We were told that very
few supplies were obtainable on the road
until we reached Nisibin, 120 miles away.

At Samarra, we had left behind a few
officers who had not sufficiently recovered
from the effects of the siege to proceed at
once on the road journey.  At Shilgat, we
picked up one officer left by the first party,
and left one or two of our own servants
behind.  All these we hoped would recover

enough to come on with the troops or subsequent parties of officers. At Mosul, we
found one of our doctors left behind by the
first party, and attending to an officer who
was down with enteric.

After a rest of two days at Mosul, we
started off on June 1 for the 200 miles to the
railhead at Ras-el-Ain. Our transport was
now composed chiefly of carts, and a few extra
carts were hired by paying in advance as
before. There was the usual uncertainty as
to how many marches it would take us, and
how many hours we should be on the road
the first day. We were now going almost
due west, and would not see our old friend
the Tigris again.

In response to our complaints to the commandant at Mosul of the way in which our
Arab escort had behaved, these men were
changed for Turkish soldiers, who gave us
less trouble. Our party was accompanied
by three magnificent Arab horses, which were
being taken to Constantinople for Enver
Pasha. The Mosul district has been the
finest horse-breeding country in Asia from the
earliest times ; indeed, it would be hard to
imagine a country better suited for the purpose than the rolling grassy plains stretching
away on both sides of the river.

After leaving the Tigris, we did not see a single tree for a hundred miles, and there was very little water of any description. The first night we spent by some dirty pools after a march of more than twenty miles. The carts were not as restful as might be imagined, since they had no springs, and every few minutes the Jehu would urge his steeds into a canter to catch up distance lost on the cart in front, or merely to try to get ahead of it. The harness was largely composed of string and rope, which often gave way, thus occasioning a long rattle for all on board before the former place in the procession was regained. Some of the horses had most appalling sores : they are evidently worked till they drop, and receive the harshest treatment from the drivers. The boys driving our carts were Kurds, wild, quick-tempered, and reckless.

The second day brought us to a camp beside a stream of pure sweet water, a welcome change after all the dirty pools and salt-laden springs which we had experienced. The following day, after a halt near some dirty springs at noon, we started on another long waterless trek in the late afternoon. We went on steadily all night, passing a large prairie fire. These fires are started to burn up the old long grass and make way for the fresh growth. They extend for miles, and at night are a fine sight, with heavy clouds of smoke hanging above.

We halted for two hours about two in the morning, and then got under way once more. About nine o'clock we came to a good stream and towards midday reached our camp at Demir Kapo. Here, there was a small river which yielded a number of fish. We saw a few Germans, and a German wireless section was camped near. We bathed in the stream, and were very glad to rest for the remainder of the day and the following morning.

Two more marches brought us to Nisibin. The country after leaving Mosul had been almost uninhabited, but here there were small villages dotted about. On getting nearer to them, we found that they were deserted; our guards told us they were Armenian villages, and that the people had all been killed earlier in the war. We passed a great many of these awful testimonies to the barbarity of Turkish politics.

Away on our right, as we approached Nisibin, could be seen Mardin, a city built on a rock overlooking the plains, and forming, as it were, a look-out from the southern fringe of the Taurus Mountains. As to how far

Mardin also was a city of the dead, it was impossible to tell. Before the war, the main Armenian population had extended from this district over a belt of land running north-eastwards up to Erzerum and Van.

At Nisibin, we camped near the river, and had a full day's rest. This place saw as much fighting as any spot in Mesopotamia in the old days, having been the frontier station between Rome and Parthia. There are not many relics of the past to be seen at the present day, but close to our bivouac stood four old pillars, bearing transverse stones which had formed part of the Roman Forum. They stood out forlornly in a field on high ground, and, as might be expected, supported a stork's nest. These birds often build a new nest on the top of one or more old ones : they are very common in Mesopotamia, and several were seen in Bagdad.

The following evening saw us moving on again, and the day after we halted at midday at Tel Erman. At this point, there is a road branching away to the north of the route we had followed and leading up to Diarbekr. The Turks were moving a good many troops at this time up to the Caucasus front, through Diarbekr, to meet the Russian pressure. We found a large camel convoy just beyond the village ; since leaving Mosul we had met no troops or convoys destined for Bagdad or the Persian front ; everything for Mesopotamia appeared to go down the Euphrates on rafts, this being the quickest way.

Tel Erman lived in our memories as being the first place where we had obtained any fruit since leaving Bagdad three weeks before. Some small cherries and apricots were to be had and were eagerly bought up.

During the evening's march, we passed a regiment of Turkish cavalry, who, for Turks, seemed to be wonderfully well equipped. The average Turk never looks happy on a horse, but these fellows made a better show than usual. As we approached the railhead at Ras-el-Ain, signs of activity increased, and there were more dead horses at the roadside, showing that the traffic was heavier.

The last day's march was one of the worst ; during the morning stage the sun was hot, there was no breeze, and quantities of sand-flies assailed us. Towards midday, we reached a big Turkish camp, where there were a good many men and stores in course of transit eastwards. Here we rested until late in the afternoon, when our final march to Ras-el-Ain began. The last few miles were accomplished at a good pace to a

F

sustained whistling accompaniment, ranging over most of the popular songs of the last few years.

Every one thought that our troubles were over, as we were now on a railway, and whatever might happen would not have to walk any farther. These hopes were dispelled a few days later, when we heard of the two breaks in the line across the Taurus Mountains, which had not yet been completed, thus necessitating two more trips by road.

We bivouacked in the open by the station, and early in the morning were told to get ready at once to go by the next train. An hour later, it appeared that we were not going till the following day. By this time we had ceased to pay much attention to Turkish orders, unless we saw that actual preparations were being made to carry them out. In the afternoon, the Turks took away all Hindu orderlies and servants, and informed us that all the doctors in our party, except one, were to stay here to look after the Indian troops on their arrival, as the latter were going to be put to work on continuing the railway farther east towards Nisibin. We were very sorry for our medical friends, since their prospects looked anything but cheerful. Local food supplied from the country round seemed almost non-existent, and the shops in the village had very little.

By the time we reached Ras-el-Ain, we had completed 200 miles from Mosul in ten days. Most of us had walked half the distance, and bumped in carts over the other half. We had kept tolerably cheerful, apart from a few inveterate grousers; altogether we had survived wonderfully well, and had fared infinitely better than the troops from Kut, who were marching along in our tracks a few days behind us.

From Ras-el-Ain we started for Aleppo the next morning, the journey taking nearly twelve hours. The only interesting place through which we passed was Jerrablus, the ancient Carchemish, where the line crosses the Euphrates by a fine bridge. There was not much sign of activity on the river banks, but before we left the station a complete train loaded with German motor-lorries had arrived, and after a few minutes continued its way eastwards.

On reaching Aleppo, in the evening, the orderlies and servants were marched off by themselves, and after loading our kit on to carts we were driven away in gharries from the station. This seemed to be almost the height of luxury, and we thought that at last we had reached a place where we should be really well treated. The gharries took us to various small hotels, but when once inside we were not allowed to go out again. The Turks said that our kit would be delivered at once; some people waited up hoping for the arrival of their valises, but the wiser seized what bedding there was obtainable in the hotel, and laying it on a veranda made the best of a bad job, and went to sleep.

In the morning, we were not allowed out to get any food. The hotel sharks refused to let boys come up with rolls, but tried to sell to us themselves at double the prices. However, we eventually got hold of a boy who threw up rolls from the street below to our veranda, and thus outwitted our enemies.

All efforts to get out for breakfast, or to fetch our kit, proved unavailing, until about midday we were allowed to go a few yards down the street to where our kit had all been thrown inside a gateway the night before. Fortunately, although a good many valises had evidently been opened, very little had been stolen.

It was not until four o'clock in the afternoon that we were finally allowed out in parties to a restaurant not a hundred yards away. While we were shut in, we had seen

Phil May in the road and shouted to him ; but, although he could see very well what we wanted, he never took the trouble to come into the hotel, much less to help us.

The next day passed in much the same fashion, except that we were allowed out at midday, and no one was sorry when we were marched off back to the station early the following morning. Here we met the orderlies, who had fared much worse than we had. The first night they had been packed into a small room in some filthy barracks, and had suffered severely from the verminous pests which flourish in every Turkish building.

A railway journey of a few hours brought us to Islahie, which was then the railhead for the journey over the Anti-Taurus range.

There were some Austrian troops in Aleppo, and we now began to meet many more Germans. Turkish training-camps were much in evidence at the stations we passed after leaving Aleppo, and a good deal of material was going south on the railway. Most of this was going to Egypt to assist in the attack which ended so disastrously for the Turks.

We spent the night at Islahie under some rough tent shelters. All our clothes had been fumigated in a steam waggon specially designed for the purpose.

The following morning we noticed a crowd of men, women, and children moving off along the road and looking very wretched. Our guards said that these were Armenians who had been working on the line, but were being taken away to make room for our troops, who would be set to work in their place; they also added that these Armenians would be marched off into a waterless spot in the hills, and kept there till they died.

We left our camp in the evening, travelling the first part of the way in carts, over one of the most bumpy roads ever seen. After a halt at the foot of the pass, we marched up, starting at midnight. There was a fine moon, and the scenery as we climbed higher became very grand. The road appeared to be only lately completed, and was probably due to German energy. As we neared the summit three or four bodies were seen lying in the ditch beside the road; these were evidently some of the Armenians we had seen starting off that morning. After descending the farther side, we bivouacked under trees in a pretty spot, and on the slope opposite saw the Armenians. Soon after they left and we did not see anything more of them. That evening we continued our way downhill, meeting several batches of sturdy Turkish youths who had just been called up and were on their way to training-camps near Aleppo. We were descending rapidly, and our drivers maintained a headlong gallop, with the result that two carts were completely overturned, but fortunately with no ill effects to the passengers. We finally bivouacked not far from the railhead, and reached the station of Mamouré early the following morning.

The railway journey across the plain, through Adana, took some six hours, bringing us to Kulek Boghaz, a station within five miles of Tarsus. From this point the road journey over the main Taurus range began. All supplies were being brought over by German motor-lorries, and everything was being run by a German commandant. During the night several helmets were stolen and probably found their way to German soldiers, who either had no sun helmets or very inferior ones. The commandant did his best to recover them, but without success. He told us that we should leave the next morning at 9 o'clock. Punctually to the minute, a dozen motor-lorries rolled up, and we were soon speeding along the road towards the mountains. The road had been cut up dreadfully by the heavy traffic, so that we were jolted about almost as badly as we had been in the Turkish carts. The scenery grew finer as we ascended, until half-way we reached an open space amongst the hills, which the Germans had made the head-quarters of their motor service, and christened " Camp Taurus." Here were enormous repair tents, one for each make of car, with living quarters and offices all of a most complete and elaborate type. After a halt here, we continued our way, still rising slowly until we entered the Cilician Gates, where the road just finds room to pass through a narrow rocky gorge. On the farther side, the descent begins at once, and is very steep in places. The road here was being repaired by bands of forced labourers, and had a much better surface.

As we neared the railway again, at Bozanti, we noticed a few British prisoners. These were naval men taken in the Dardanelles. They said they were being paid, and apparently had not much to complain about. We were not allowed to stop and speak to them, and can only hope that they fared better than our own troops who were put to work shortly afterwards on the neighbouring sections of the line through the Taurus.

At Bozanti, we were able to buy a few stores, some of which were British and had been left behind at Gallipoli when we evacuated the peninsula. With only a short wait, we were packed like sardines into a train, and the next stage of the journey began.

The next morning we reached Konia, and were told to leave the train, but not to take our kit out, as the train was stopping for some time. The local commandant arrived, and proved to be the best Turkish officer we had met. Under his direction, we were taken to a hospital building, where there were two large rooms containing rough beds. These were a great delight after sleeping on the ground for weeks. The commandant, a little later, decided that we should be allowed to remain here until the next day, so that we might have a rest. If we had relied on Phil May, our kit would have all gone on in the afternoon to Constantinople, but luckily we just managed to rescue it in time.

The greatest delight of Konia, from our point of view, was an hotel near the station, to which we were allowed to go for meals. This was run by a Frenchwoman, who was kindness itself, and could not do enough for us. Few of us will forget the delights of her omelets or the hot baths in a real long bath, the first we had seen since leaving India.

The journey next day was more comfortable, as we had more room. After spending another night in the train, we arrived in the morning at Afion Kara Hissar, where a good number of Gallipoli prisoners were interned. In the evening, we reached Eski Chehir, the junction for the Angora line. Here all our Mohammedan servants were taken from us. We were conducted a little way into the town to the houses where a number of Indian Mohammedan officers, who had come along with the first party, were living. They seemed to have fared pretty well, and certainly had very good quarters. They were very glad to see us, and we anxiously inquired after their experiences by the way.

Up to this point we had fondly imagined that Angora would be the end of our journey, but just before starting in the evening we were told that another ten days by road lay in front of us after reaching Angora. We were packed tight in the train, and rumbled on slowly through the night, arriving at Angora at eleven o'clock next day. Our kit was left to be brought in carts, while we were marched through the town to a big building over a mile beyond. This had been built as an Agricultural College, but latterly used as a Military School. Here we found the first party of officers, whom we had last seen at Shamrán camp. They seemed to have had a much more unpleasant journey than we had; whether it was because they had most of the staff officers amongst them, or had adopted the plan of telling every Turk and interpreter exactly what they thought of them, certain it is that they were not enjoying life, and when we arrived had not been allowed outside the building for two whole days.

We had bidden farewell to Phil May with great delight at Eski Chehir, and had since then been in charge of a much pleasanter officer. Thanks to his efforts, we succeeded in getting permission to stay out of doors to cook and to go down to a neighbouring stream to bathe in the evening. We felt that the first party really owed us a great debt of gratitude in thus providing them with an opportunity of washing and getting a little fresh air.

All our orderlies had been marched off from the station to some dirty Turkish barracks, so that we were entirely dependent on our own culinary efforts. Two days after our arrival, the first party left in carts for Yozgad, a distance of 100 miles due east on the road to Sivas and Erzerum. We remained for a week, being only allowed to go into the town once to make purchases. The journey to Kastamuni began under the best conditions. The weather was perfect, and as we were well over 2,000 feet above sea-level the sun was never too hot at midday. Also, we had a new commandant, who did what he could to help us. The distance in front of us was 140 miles, and we expected to take fully a week.

The road led through countless orchards for the first few miles, and then on into more open country. Cherries and small apricots abounded, and supplies in general were plentiful; a very different state of affairs existed a year later, when prices had doubled and trebled, and in many cases advanced very much more. We reached a small village the first evening, and our commandant appeared much surprised that we should prefer to sleep in the open rather than in the very doubtful shelters attached to the local resthouse.

The following day we reached Kalejik, a picturesque little place with the ruins of an old castle perched on a rocky pinnacle in the centre of the town. Some such ruin seems to keep watch over all Turkish towns. We had already seen similar old forts perched on hills at Afion Kara Hissar and Angora.

Next morning, most of our carts were taken away, and we were given donkeys instead. A small moke cannot keep pace with a cart, and it is an open question whether riding the animal with a loading saddle is less fatiguing than walking along and driving it in front of one. Provided all one's kit had been put on a cart, the easiest way was often to let the moke go where it liked, and walk on oneself without it.

Two days from Kalejik brought us to Changri, a prettily situated little place, which came suddenly into view, as we rounded a bend in the road, after traversing a very desolate and uninteresting stretch of country all day. We bivouacked under some trees by a stream, which, however, was not fit to drink from. The local commandant and Town Council paid us a visit. We were allowed to visit the bazaar, and generally made ourselves comfortable.

In the morning, we were given more carts again, much to our delight, and continued our way northward. The road now began to cross some high ridges. On one of these we passed a police post, and a halt was made while our commandant stalked a few sitting pigeons with his shot-gun, eventually securing one after a great deal of trouble. Beyond sand-grouse, between Bagdad and Mosul, we had seen very little game of any sort since we left Kut.

We camped by a stream, after a very steep and bumpy descent from a high ridge. It is extraordinary what treatment the light Turkish transport carts can stand without anything giving way.

Our next march led us up a very long ascent, and proved the most enjoyable day of our whole journey. After ascending some distance, the road entered pine woods, and reminded us very strongly of roads near different hill stations in India. We halted at midday very near the top of the pass, which must be close on 4,000 feet, while the mountains on either side rise to another 2,000 feet. The views were glorious, and we wished it might have been possible to stay longer in such scenery. By evening, we had dropped down a long distance on the other side and were nearly out of the woods again when we halted for our last bivouac.

We were now within ten miles of Kastamuni, and by eleven o'clock next morning, July 5th, were in sight of the place. The old castle, standing on its rocky crest, was the first sight which greeted us as we looked down into the valley from the top of the ridge along which we had come. The town, spreading up and down the valley round the base of the castle rock, seemed very much larger than any Turkish town we had seen since leaving Aleppo. The valley was green with culti- vated fields and trees, while the hillsides were bare and brown.

We were halted just outside the town, while a number of local gendarmes formed up on each side of the road. After a long wait, we thus progressed in state into the town and through the bazaar to our quarters, which proved to be houses from which the former Greek inhabitants had been ejected. In the end, although somewhat crowded, we found ourselves each with a bed, bedding, and a little other furniture. Most of us had not slept in a bed for eight months or more, apart perhaps from a few days in hospital, and all we desired at the moment was one long rest.

During the last week, which had been by far the pleasantest of the whole trek, we had averaged twenty miles a day. Our journey altogether had been nearly 1,700 miles, and was probably the longest distance across country any prisoners of war have had to travel to the place of their confinement.

# CHAPTER IV

## LIFE IN KASTAMUNI

### *July* 1916—*August* 1917

ON arrival in Kastamuni, we were divided into two groups, one being accommodated in a large building, formerly a Greek school, with one or two adjacent houses, and the other in a number of houses in a street lower down the hill. Both places were on the edge of the town in the Greek quarter. The schoolhouse was perched high up and commanded a splendid view across the town in the valley towards the hills, beyond which lay the Black Sea—only some 40 miles away.

The houses were built up on a wooden frame-work, the bricks being thrown in to fill up the intervening spaces in a most casual manner. The best houses were covered with stucco ; but, however good in appearance, each house in Turkey has its own numerous population of small inhabitants. An Austrian lady whom we met assured us that her house was the only one in the town free from these pests, and we could well believe it.

The town itself is shut in by the valley and presents a confused jumble of houses, with almost innumerable mosques, and in the centre one or two large Government buildings. The mosques are not particularly beautiful, there being no golden domes or blue tilework. The most pretentious have plain grey stone minarets, while the smaller ones have to be content with little steeples of wood. During Ramazan a ring of lights is kept burning at night round each minaret, and gives the town a strange appearance, as these are the only lights showing, there being no such thing as street lamps, and very few lights in private houses—with kerosine at a prohibitive price.

After the weary march from Kut, we were only too delighted to get into our new quarters, and sleeping in a bed again was a luxury not soon to be forgotten. A restaurant had been arranged, and we found a very good meal ready for us soon after arrival. Unfortunately, this was much the best repast we obtained from the contractor, and when it came to arranging a daily messing scheme we had to be content with

G

a very moderate programme. However, every one had got so tired of scraping along, cooking and foraging for themselves on the journey up, that any sort of plan by which some one else would do the work was not to be refused, even if we were to be done over it.

During the summer of 1916, food in the town was comparatively cheap, eggs being a halfpenny each or less, and good white flour about sixpence a pound. Fruit was to be had in prolific quantities, the cherries being especially good. But no one takes any trouble to cultivate fruit in this part of Turkey. There are grapes, melons, peaches, apples and pears in great profusion, but all of the commonest kind. Had the country any communications worth the name, no doubt it would be different, but, as it is, the Turk is content with what grows by itself and does not need any special attention. The local taste in over-ripe and bad pears was most surprising. For weeks one would see baskets of rotting pears in the bazaar on market days and the country people enjoying them.

The ruined castle on its rocky pinnacle must have dated back to very early times ; it is now used as a " look-out " station and has three ancient guns, which are fired as an alarm in case of fire and at other moments of importance, such as the first sight of the new moon at the end of Ramazan. The greatest wonder to us was that the whole town had not been burnt down long ago, since all the bazaar houses were wooden and dry as tinder. The fire brigade consisted of one prehistoric manual pump which was carried about on the shoulders of five or six youths, with a scratch collection of hose and buckets. On one occasion a major of the S. & T. Corps was so overcome with laughter on seeing this apparition that the commandant, feeling much insulted, had him confined to the house for a fortnight.

This was our first commandant, a very ignorant specimen, who, so report said, had been a farmer in the Caucasus. He was a most depressing sight at all times. Most Turkish officers only shave on Thursdays, and he was no exception to the rule. His trousers invariably swept the ground ; he always wore goloshes several sizes too large and an old overcoat. He would shuffle about with his hands in his pockets, his shoulders hunched up, looking the picture of misery. Yet, notwithstanding his apparent dejection, he was making quite a good thing out of us, as we found out later on. The restaurant contractor was paying him about

£30 a month, and, between them, they were charging us rent for our quarters, which was quite contrary to all rules. Another little source of income was making us each pay for a 5-piastre receipt stamp for our monthly pay instead of a $2\frac{1}{2}$d.

This commandant knew no language except Turkish, and consequently an interpreter was needed on all occasions. At the start this was a Greek, who made great protestations of his friendliness to us ; but we very soon found him to be a double-faced blackguard doing his best to make a good thing out of us by arranging for commissions with the shopkeepers with whom we dealt.

Fortunately for us, early in 1917, a Turkish colonel—Zeur Bey, from Constantinople—arrived unexpectedly on a visit of inspection, with the result that the commandant was promptly dismissed and matters regarding overcharges for house rent put right. The commandant was said to have been seen on his knees before the colonel imploring forgiveness. This at all events was the story of Sherif Bey, the second in command, who was by way of being very anxious to do all he could for us. On our march from Angora to Kastamuni he had certainly done his best for us, but later on we were forced to distrust him.

Turkish officers, as a rule, have very good manners and promise one almost anything without the least idea of ever keeping their word. They speak French with a very good accent, which makes one give them credit for knowing a great deal more of that language than is usually the case. It is quite impossible to describe the uniforms worn by officers, as one so seldom sees two dressed alike. All material being so scarce and expensive, uniforms were made from almost anything, and there being no such person as a provost-marshal no one could interfere. Consequently, one saw some officers dressed in a highly picturesque style, looking as if they had just been taking a part in " The Chocolate Soldier " or " The Balkan Princess," and others whom one could only recognize from shopkeepers by their badges of rank.

The Greek interpreter was the first one of the original staff to depart. After him, two very much better fellows were sent us. One of these was a young Turk named Remzi, who had been a naval cadet in Constantinople when the war broke out—and still cherished the fond hope of one day being an officer in the British Navy, for which he had the most profound veneration. Unfortunately, in trying to help us, he wrote to Constantinople ;

got into trouble with his seniors, and was sent away. We were thus left with the second man, an Armenian, who was always called " Napoleon " from his likeness to the Great Man. Napoleon was very cautious, but, considering the difficulty of his own position, he did us very well.

After our first commandant had disappeared, his successor arrived in the shape of a very small, but very stout and cheery little man, named Fattah Bey. He proved to be a very good fellow and things were soon running much more pleasantly. A great point in his favour was that he spoke German, and we were thus able to dispense with an interpreter. Capt. H., of the I.A.R.O., took charge of him on most occasions, and after we had had him a few weeks he was becoming quite pro-British.

The greatest events in our life were undoubtedly the arrival of a mail or parcels. The letters we received in July 1916, soon after our arrival, were the first news most of us had had from our friends at home since before the siege began in Kut nearly eight months earlier. On an average, letters came through every ten days or so, the quickest time taken from home, via Switzerland, Vienna and Constantinople, being 25 days.

Parcels travelled by the same route, but were very much longer in making their appearance. At first they arrived in three to four months, but gradually took longer and longer, until finally they were eight and nine months on the way. The reason for this delay was to be found in Vienna, where all parcels were transhipped, and apparently thrown into a depot until such time as the Austrian officials decided to send a few more on. Any big operations on the Italian front had the immediate effect of stopping all parcels and sometimes letters as well. There were exceedingly few cases of anything having been actually stolen and, up to a certain date, officers had received nearly all parcels sent from home.

Soon after our arrival, we received a number of gifts through the American Embassy in Constantinople, who were at that time looking after our interests. These consisted of thin cotton things for the summer, and, when wearable, were of considerable use. Unfortunately, they were much too small, and it was a very lucky man who could wear the trousers he was given. Later on, more clothes arrived, these being thick winter garments which, although not providing the same amount of amusement, fitted us better and were a great godsend, since it was not until the New Year that people began to receive the clothes they wanted from home.

The winter in Kastamuni and, in fact, over most of Asia Minor can be very severe ; but it is a dry and healthy cold. In February 1917, we had well over 20 degrees of frost for days, and during the following winter the temperature at Changri went down to 6 degrees below zero. Indeed, it would have been hard to find a better climate than Kastamuni, which was 2,500 feet above the sea. The rainfall there was very small and confined almost entirely to March and April. The summer temperature was very much the same as in England, but drier.

As one gets nearer to the Black Sea coast, the rainfall increases and the vegetation gets thicker. Between Angora and Changri there are wide stretches of almost desert land. At Kastamuni we had pine woods and shrubs on the hills, while all the valleys were extensively irrigated. On the Black Sea coast itself the climate is much milder in winter and there are thick woods of beech, oak and fir with heavy undergrowth.

Apart from the kitchen, which always has a huge open chimney, there were no fireplaces of the ordinary kind in the houses. All heating in winter is done by stoves of sheet iron with a chimney leading out through the nearest wall. These stoves, fed with wood, give out a tremendous heat for a short time, but it is very hard to maintain anything approaching an even temperature. Wood was plentiful during the winter of 1916-17, and we used to buy it in the form of whole logs. These we had sawn up by two Armenians into short lengths, which we then split with an axe. This gave us a good deal of exercise during the cold winter mornings. Unfortunately, the next year, wood had become scarce and much more expensive and all prisoners suffered considerably in consequence. A good deal of charcoal is used for cooking, but we saw no coal being used in the district, even the railway up to Angora being largely dependent on wood.

After a few months at the restaurant, the contractor began to put up prices and most of us demurred. This finally led to the majority going on strike and deciding to mess themselves, as we were allowed to by the rules. The old commandant, however, and the contractor, had no idea of accepting the alternative if they could possibly help it. Consequently, we were first forbidden to cook in the kitchens of our own houses, for fear we should set the chimneys and the houses on fire. To get over this, we made fireplaces in the back gardens or yards behind the houses. Other little pin-pricks of the same kind were tried, but we finally got our own way, and found that our mess bills were reduced to nearly a half what they had been before. We had a number of British orderlies with us, who did our cooking and waited on us. To start with, there was some difficulty in getting a separate room as a dining-room for each mess, but eventually we settled down and furnished on an economical plan, our carpenters making benches, tables, etc.

The restaurant contractor was so disgusted at our strike that he closed down altogether for two or three days, thus throwing out into the cold the few who had remained faithful to him on any conditions rather than do their own catering. There was, somewhat naturally, a good deal of ill-feeling between the two parties in consequence, and it took time to die out. In the end, the restaurant supporters had to start a mess of their own and came into line with the rest of us.

We were allowed a fair amount of liberty, although at the start things did not look promising, the old commandant telling us we should be only able to go one short walk a week. Actually we were allowed in the road for a hundred yards or so outside our houses and could go to the bazaar or Turkish bath any day by getting a sentry to go with us.

The Hamáms, or Turkish baths, of which there are a great many, are not the elaborately furnished places one sees at home, but consist of two vaulted chambers, supplied with vapour. Round the side are ledges on which one sits, and stone basins with a supply of hot and cold water. After being stewed in the hottest chamber for a quarter of an hour, one passes out to the outer room, where an aged attendant is generally ready to operate with buckets of cold water. Next one proceeds to the dressing-rooms and reclines comfortably swathed in towels, while Turkish coffee is brought round. After the first few months, sugar became so expensive that it was no longer provided, and the coffee seemed very poor in consequence. Altogether, in a place where one had plenty of time to spare, the Hamám provided a very pleasant way of spending a morning.

The Turks used to put up numbers of rules for our benefit. These were written out in the best English the interpreter could achieve, which was never very clear. As a rule, we did not pay very much attention to them, and they, on the other hand, never seemed to care either. The rule was on the board, and, if any officious officer was to come round from Constantinople, he could always be shown it, and assured it was strictly obeyed.

On one occasion a notice was suddenly put up, informing us that all lights henceforth must be put out at 9.30 p.m. It was thought advisable to do so the first night ; the second night, the time was about 9.45 ; and after that we continued to go to bed when we pleased, and were never bothered any more about it.

Owing to the tremendously high price of kerosine, Daylight Saving soon came into force, and saved us a great deal.

The sentries, on the whole, were a very good-natured lot and would never have worried us with restrictions as far as they themselves were concerned. They were mostly old men who had served in previous wars and, until called up, were living on their own small farms. One of the best of them was " Johnnie Walker," a little man who had a most extraordinary stride and could walk any of us to a standstill. We always tried to get him when going for a long walk, knowing that from personal motives he would never stop us going a good distance. Another favourite was " Ginger," a very harmless old fellow with sandy whiskers. As one went past, he would lean over and whisper confidentially : " Ginger fennah ? "—Is Ginger a bad fellow ? Every now and then they went to their homes on leave and came back with a few pounds of butter or a bag of wheatmeal, which they sold to us without much difficulty.

On our arrival, the only weapons the guard possessed were ancient pinfire rifles, firing a huge lump of lead. Each man had exactly two rounds in his possession. Later on some rather younger men came, armed with captured Russian rifles.

We soon managed to hire a field for football. It was very stony and by no means level, but, nevertheless, was a great acquisition. As a rule, each group of houses used it three days a week. To start with, we only had a Soccer case and no bladder. We stuffed the case with grass and played a very modified form of Rugger, where collaring was disallowed on account of the stones, and punting and place kicking forbidden in order to preserve the life of the ball. After some weeks we got some proper footballs from Constantinople, and others came eventually from home. We played matches against the other group of houses, Regulars *v*. Irregulars, and every other thing we could think of. Soccer Sixes caused much excitement and a local firm of bookmakers, who came into existence for the occasion, did a large business.

We could always rely on getting out somewhere every day. During the early summer we had splendid walks two days a week over the hills in the mornings. These long walks did not suit everybody, and a gentle form of meandering had to be organized for the " slugs." On one celebrated occasion, we walked out about five miles, taking our lunch, and had a very cheery picnic, but this was never allowed again, and in July 1917 all long walks were suddenly stopped, and we were barely allowed outside the boundaries of the town.

For news of the outer world, we were dependent upon the local telegrams, which the best Turkish scholars used to translate, and also upon the " Hilal," a German-run paper, printed in Constantinople. This paper, of which we used to receive the French Edition, had been started for propaganda purposes at the beginning of the war. The news was, naturally, very one-sided, but, reading between the lines, one could tell fairly well what was the position on the Western Front.

In addition, we had maps, and could follow
the places mentioned, when, as during the
Somme offensive, the Germans, " according
to our preconceived plan," took up a position
some miles in rear of their last. A serial
story which ran for some time in this paper
was called " L'évadé de Tsingtau," and gave
the adventures of a German, who having
escaped from Tsingtau after the Japanese
had taken it, reached America, was caught
while trying to cross to Germany, spent some
time in Donnington Hall, but finally succeeded in escaping, and swam off from near
Tilbury to a Dutch ship lying in the river,
thus getting clear away. Whether true or not,
it made a wonderful story.

News carefully camouflaged in our letters
from home invariably arrived safely ; in fact,
the Turks never troubled to censor anything
in the letters we received. On the other
hand, every now and then some officious
creature in Constantinople would systematically cut up our long letters, which we were
allowed to write twice a month, and only send
on the first two and last two lines.

There were always plenty of rumours
amongst the Greek shopkeepers in the bazaar.
For instance, we were told the British had
taken Bagdad long before they did, and our

troops in Palestine were always said to be within three or four marches of Aleppo ; the Russians were just outside Sivas, and Trieste had been taken by the Italians. The Turks themselves never believed these stories, and, in fact, even when the armistice was signed, many of them in country districts had not heard that Bagdad was in our possession. They received no letters from their friends at the front, no casualty lists were published, and the only news that seemed to reach them by post was a few letters from Turks we had taken to Burma as prisoners, who seemed to be very happy and contented.

The country people never showed any " hate " against us, but the authorities used to make this an excuse for curtailing our walks, saying how fanatical the village people were in the neighbourhood.

Apart from football matches, we employed ourselves in various ways. There were soon two or three well-established firms of carpenters, who did a great deal of work and made a lot of furniture. Others took to cobbling, and had plenty to do to keep our boots in order. A good many studied various languages, but Turkish was not very popular, as no one expected ever to want it again when once they had left the country.

We had quite a good library, and books came through without much trouble in parcels from home.

A long series of lectures were held during the winter, every one who could do so lecturing to the rest of us. It is wonderful what a comprehensive programme can be formed when one is really put to it.

Another intellectual effort was a debating society; but this did not have a very long life.

Our greatest achievement was undoubtedly the band. This was started in the spring of 1917, under the auspices of our new commandant, who was very keen about it. At first there were only two or three violins which had been discovered in the bazaar, then others were found, also some clarionets; drums and banjos were soon made, and, finally—greatest triumph of all—two 'cellos and a double bass were manufactured by our most progressive firm of carpenters. Altogether, the band numbered about sixteen. At the start they had no music, and Lieut. Parsons, R.F.A., who conducted, had to score the parts for a number of pieces, most of which were wonderfully successful. Later on, music came from home, and concerts were given twice a week.

We even had a little dancing on one or two

H

occasions, and one day the commandant brought two or three Greek and Armenian ladies. This was such a success that he became very excited and declared " Next veek plenty lady kom." Life seemed to be improving all round, but it was too good to last, and suddenly everything was stopped. The commandant got into hot water with the other Turkish authorities in the town, who had probably reported him behind his back to Constantinople. Our walks were suddenly curtailed and no long walks allowed. Had the little man been able to stand up for himself, things would have been much better, but he was much too scared to take a strong line, and a few days later departed for Eski-Chehir to take the place of the commandant there, who, in turn, was to come to Kastamuni.

During the winter of 1916, prices began to rise rapidly in the bazaar and this went on all through 1917, until in 1918 all prisoners had great difficulty in getting food, even in the new camps, which were said to be better off in this respect than Kastamuni.

When we first arrived, there was a small amount of silver money in circulation, the smallest notes which were just being introduced being 20 and 5 piastres—3s. 4d. and

10d. in ordinary times. Not long afterwards, these were followed by 2½ and 1 piastre notes, which carried pictures of the Dardanelles and Kut on the back, Kut being quite unrecognizable. For smaller change recourse had to be taken to stamps and by midsummer of 1917 no coins of any sort were to be seen.

Money came through to us in various ways, but the best exchange we could get was by cashing undated cheques with the Greek shopkeepers in the town, who gave us 160 piastres to the pound, whereas through the Dutch Embassy we could only get 140, the exchange rate before the war being 112. The shopkeepers would not be able to cash these cheques till the end of the war, and it says something for the reputation of a British cheque that they would accept them on such conditions. They undoubtedly regarded such cheques as being a very much safer asset than the Turkish paper money, which was the only alternative, and, at the end of the war, would very likely be suddenly repudiated by a paternal Government.

We were paid by the Turks at the rate they pay their own officers, the equivalent of this being deducted from our accounts by the War Office.

On the way up from Kut we were given one month's pay in Bagdad, which for senior officers was on a comparatively generous scale. However, on reaching Kastamuni, these unfortunates were told that the Bagdad rates were quite wrong, and they were now to pay up the difference ; this took several months in many cases.

Happily for us, soon after our arrival, the Red Cross came to our assistance, working through the American Embassy in Constantinople. They gave us £T.3 a month, which, with a subaltern's allowance of £T.7 as pay from the Turks, made it just possible to carry on.

As food got more expensive, the Red Cross increased their allowance to £T.5 a month, and had finally to increase this still further.

In May and June 1917, some additional orderlies arrived ; these men had been in other camps up till then, and were not all Kut prisoners, some having been taken in the Dardanelles and others in Egypt. They brought dreadful stories of the treatment of the troops during the first few months, and it became clear that at least two-thirds of the Kut garrison were already dead. The last news they had heard was that all fit prisoners were being sent back to the North of Syria to work on the railway there. As conditions were very bad in that district when we came through in 1916, no one can say what those who returned a year later had to go through. This area was considered as one under military operations, and was, therefore, excluded from the agreement finally come to by which the Dutch Embassy in Constantinople was to inspect the various camps.

Unfortunately, some of these new orderlies contracted typhus on their way to Kastamuni, at one of the dirty halting-places, and three succumbed. They were buried beside three officers whom we had already laid to rest, in a little cemetery at the top of the hill overlooking the town, near the slope where the Greeks and Armenians are buried. Wooden crosses were at first put up over the graves, but these were at once torn up and stolen by the Turkish peasants. We then obtained heavy slabs of stone, on which a cross was carved and the names cut. A wall was built round the little spot, a number of officers going up every morning and working hard until it was completed. Now that no British prisoners are left in Kastamuni, one hopes that the little cemetery will be allowed to remain undisturbed on the bare hillside.

During the summer of 1917, a number of officers were in favour of getting the Turks to move the camp from Kastamuni to some place nearer to the railway, as it was thought that it would then be easier to obtain supplies of wood and fuel during the coming winter. It is doubtful if this would have been the case, but an official request was sent to Constantinople. Towards the end of July 1917, our liberties were considerably curtailed for no apparent reason, and after the escape of our party, on August 8th, very severe restrictions were imposed.

Nowhere in Turkey could life in 1917-18 be considered amenable, since food was so short in all districts. This, combined with the depreciation in the paper money, kept prices very high and made messing a great problem ; if parcels could have got through more quickly from home it would have made a big difference.

At the end of September, the first batch of officers was moved to Changri, and the remainder followed early in October. At Changri accommodation was provided in a dirty Turkish barrack, which, besides needing very extensive cleansing, required much glass in the windows. Shortly afterwards, two-thirds of the officers left for Gedos, a small place about a hundred miles east of Smyrna, where they were placed on parole, and given liberty to go where they pleased unguarded. The remainder stayed for some months at Changri, where they had managed to make themselves fairly comfortable, although only allowed to go out to a neighbouring field for exercise.    Later, however, they were sent to Yozgad, the camp to which the first half of the Kut officers had originally been sent.

# CHAPTER V

## ESCAPE FROM KASTAMUNI

RETURNING to events in Kastamuni, in November 1916 a little more housing accommodation had become available for us, and as a result I found myself sharing a good room with Keeling, a lieutenant in the I.A.R.O. One evening, soon afterwards, I asked him if he would make an effort with me to reach the Russians if, as we hoped, they should advance further west from their lines, which were then running due south to Erzinjan from a point a little way west of Trebizond. He replied that he had long been thinking of it, and had made a start towards preparing for such an effort by carefully preserving two 1 lb. tins of chocolate which he had received from home!

At that time such a journey meant a distance of 300 miles across country from Kastamuni, and we considered it quite hopeless in view of the mountainous country to be passed. It was also obvious that any attempt to get a long distance across country would stand a much better chance if made in the summer time. It would be impossible to carry enough food and we should have to fall back on such crops, fruit and vegetables as might be ripe and obtainable. We thought April or May would be the earliest possible month. Another alternative was to get to the coast, only 38 miles as the crow flies, and then to steal a boat. This necessitated having one man in the party who knew how to sail a boat, and added a big risk in the very fact of having to launch a boat secretly and get away from a coast which as far as we could hear was well guarded.

The general opinion was that it was quite hopeless to try to get away. This belief was shared by the senior officers and, under pressure from the Turkish commandant, most people gave their parole not to try to escape under present conditions. About ten of us refused : some because they believed such an act was definitely against Army rules, and the others, like ourselves, because they hoped for a chance to get away and considered that they were justified in taking such a chance if it seemed to offer any possibility of success. Pressure was brought to bear upon us by the Turks to change our views ; but we remained firm. We were told our liberty would be curtailed ; we would be put in a separate house by ourselves ; while the others were to get additional liberty. What actually happened was exactly nothing, and we all went on precisely as before. It appeared to be merely a dodge on the part of the Turks to save themselves trouble and responsibility. From time to time, owing to various good reasons, many others withdrew their parole, and by the date we departed—August 8th, 1917—nearly half the officers must have followed suit.

In the meanwhile K. and I had been trying to collect information and had been sounding a few other officers. It was very hard to get anything which was at all trustworthy : some reports said there were no boats on the coast, others that a boat could probably be obtained. One Greek told us that it would be impossible to get through to the Russian lines, as the people east of Samsun were so wild and savage. This man was making plenty of money out of us in his professional capacity, and evidently did not wish any disturbances between us and the Turks to imperil his tranquillity and source of gain. We were not therefore much influenced by his fears.

Maps were a necessity, and the only one we

had was on a scale of 32 miles to an inch. I made tracings of this, so as to have duplicate copies, but the scale was too small to be of much use beyond showing the general trend of the country. I also succeeded in making a compass of a rough description by fixing a dial to some magnetic needles and suspending it with a thread. Fortunately, however, a little later, we discovered a shop in the town where we could buy some cheap but tolerably serviceable compasses, and secured several of these, taking care that the sentry with us did not see what we were buying. The best map we had seen was hanging up in our commandant's office. This was a German one and to a scale of about seven miles to an inch. No opportunity occurred, unfortunately, of being able to copy it. It showed us, however, a large number of farms and villages sprinkled over the countryside. The Russians had advanced no further, and the only plan at all feasible seemed to be to get a boat on the coast and make for Trebizond.

As the summer began our discussions took a more practical shape, and we got in touch with people who were in a position to know something trustworthy. One of those we approached was an interned Ally. Under various pretexts I succeeded in getting a sentry to come with me to his house, which was strictly against the rules, saying I wanted to buy a guitar. On arrival he produced the guitar, and while pretending to try it we discussed the possibility of getting away. He considered that it would be possible to get a boat on the coast at Ineboli and suggested sending someone he could trust to find out how things stood and if possible to make arrangements. Conversation was not too easy, as his knowledge of English was very sketchy and I knew nothing of his language ; also the sentry was present, so that everything had to appear to be about the guitar and no names of places mentioned aloud. A little money and cigarettes to the sentry ensured his not talking later about where we had been, and I endeavoured to get the same man on the next occasion. One day at this house I met a fellow countryman who as a civilian had been interned at Constantinople. For some reason the Turks had become more suspicious and he had been packed off to Kastamuni. He gave me some useful information about the state of the country further east, but was not at all hopeful of our getting through. I did not see him again, as he was naturally very loth to be seen speaking to any of us, as that would mean his being sent out to live in one of the small villages away from every vestige of civilization. Meanwhile K. had been interviewing one or two people whom we thought might be trusted. For this purpose an appointment was generally made at the Hamám, or Turkish bath. We were allowed to go to these baths, of which there were a large number in the town, whenever we liked, and, as the sentry always stayed in the entrance hall, one could speak freely to anyone inside. On the whole these Allies recommended us not to make any attempt, one saying that had it been possible he himself would of course have gone long ago. Actually, they were afraid of trying anything of the sort or being in any way implicated by us.

We discussed the proposal of my friend with some of the others and decided to try his suggestion. Accordingly ten of us collected about 50 liras—one lira equals 18s. 6d. nominally—which was handed to him. He in turn was to arrange with a Greek who was going to the coast and promised to bring back the information we needed. After some delay he finally departed, and, as we had feared, never turned up again.

Some of those who had subscribed considered any attempt without previously obtaining a boat to be hopeless and, when the Greek never returned, the number who were keen to go was reduced to half a dozen. Much discussion followed as to the size of the party, whether there should be two parties and who should go in which, and what routes should be followed. Eventually only four of us prepared to start, the others promising to give us all the support they could. Our party now consisted of Captains R. J. Tipton, R.F.C., R. T. Sweet, 2/7th Ghurkas, Lieut. E. H. Keeling, and myself, both of the I.A.R.O. " Tip " had been taken in Egypt, while we three had all been in Kut.

There were two possible ways of getting out of the camp, or rather away from the street in which we lived, and either seemed fairly easy to arrange.

In order to get our provisions ready, we had to take one or two of the British orderlies into our confidence. We decided after much scheming that we would take 20 lb. of food each, consisting of 11 lb. of biscuits, 2½ lb. of cheese, 2½ lb. of smoked meat, 1¾ lb. of chocolate, 1½ lb. of Horlick's Malted Milk and the remainder of soup squares, cocoa and sugar, with a box of tea tabloids. The biscuits were made of good white flour, for which we had at that time to pay an exorbitant price as it was almost unobtainable ; butter and sugar, which were also appallingly expensive, were added. Some were made with raisins, all being baked as hard as possible to save weight. These, with raisins, proved much the most popular subsequently. Our mess cook, Gunner Prosser, R.F.A., made most of the biscuits and was very keen to do all he could to help us. In order to keep things dark we told as few people as possible, but several people must have suspected us before we finally took our departure. The all-important question of the food to be carried caused much discussion before the final schedule was drawn up. Some were for taking one solid lump of duff instead of biscuits, but the latter won the day as containing less water and being therefore of more value weight for weight. K. had a profound belief in Horlick's Malted Milk, which was fully justified by our subsequent experience. For some days prior to our departure a notice on the board, which was used by people who wished to exchange contents of parcels from home, informed all and sundry that Lt. K. could offer a very large variety of articles, ranging from honey to socks, in exchange for Malted Milk. This resulted in most of our supply being obtained. The question of meat was difficult, as tinned stuff received from home was too heavy and there was nothing to be got in the bazaar but smoked mutton, which was not very appetizing. Eventually, we decided on the mutton. We had a good many soup squares of different kinds, but on the journey we wished we had had more cocoa instead. We decided to pack as much food as possible in small bags, for which some puggaree cloth came in handy, and an old pillow-case made a good receptacle for the biscuits. K. spent a long time sewing up small bags and in generally thinking out and preparing for all eventualities.

In the event of our being forced to buy food, we had decided that our only chance was to pretend we were Germans, since the country people, while seeing we were not Turks, would be too ignorant to know any difference between Briton and Hun. This also fell in well with our plan of going in uniform. To make things more secure we forged a passport. This was written out by Captain Rich, 120th Infantry, who knew Turkish fairly well, and purported to be a letter from the Army commander at Angora to Hauptmann Hermann von Below, who, with three German orderlies, was said to be travelling on a surveying expedition. It was requested that the utmost facilities should be given him in his work. The name of the Army commander we had managed to obtain correctly, and this was signed in a different hand and ink. A seal was also appended, as is usual in all Turkish documents, and suitably smudged so that the name which did not correspond with the signature might be illegible.

A volume dealing with woodcraft was perused by K., who discovered that the ordinary type of rock lichen was a highly nutritious food and, also, that nearly all forms of toadstool were equally useful. We hoped not to need such emergency rations and, fortunately, never got to that stage in our subsequent adventures. Over and above the 20 lb. of food we estimated that each one would need to carry 10 lb. more in kit and equipment, the former comprising a spare pair of socks, a " woolly " and vest or something similar, and the latter a haversack and waterbottle, matches, knife, spoon and soap. In addition we carried a sail, about 40 feet of light rope, a light axe head, two canteens, a safety razor, housewife, nails and thread for repairing boots, maps, and compasses. These were divided up into equal weights between the four of us. The sail was rather a work of art. It was made in two pieces from a bed sheet, the lining of two Wolseley valises and a couple

I

of towels. With the help of a sailor friend, Lieut. Nicholson, R.N.R., we roped it all round. It measured about 10 ft. by 7 ft. 6 in., and weighed complete about 7 lb. The idea was that, having discovered a boat and if need be hewn down a small tree for a mast, we would paddle off from the coast and put up the sail as quickly as possible after sewing the two pieces together. Tip was to be our navigator, as he had done a good deal of sailing in pre-war days.

As Sweet was the only man with a rucksack, we three had to make our own. This meant a good deal of laborious sewing. My own was laid on the foundation of a khaki drill bag originally received in Mesopotamia with gifts from the ladies of Bombay; this was reinforced with an old pair of braces and the necessary webbing sewn on. It proved a most useful article and stood the journey wonderfully well, although getting somewhat soiled in appearance.

# CHAPTER VI

## THE FIRST NIGHT

IT was not the easiest thing in the world to hold our meetings, accomplish our sewing and complete the sail without being interrupted by other people or giving the show away. Our excuses for keeping many people out of our room must have seemed rather thin on many occasions, and certainly gave rise to suspicion in one quarter. One day the interpreter Napoleon came to the door, but luckily suspected nothing and departed. Napoleon had been of great service to us after the wretched Greek interpreter we had had on our arrival, and we hoped our departure would not get him into trouble. We instructed our orderly to endeavour to put Napoleon off the track the morning after we had gone. The rule was that we had to report to him at ten in the morning as well as at night. Very often people omitted to do so, but in that case he generally wandered round quietly until he had seen they were still present. Our confederates amongst the officers promised to say we had all gone up the hill to work at the cemetery to which a party went every day, to complete the building of a wall round the graves of the three officers and three men whom we had there laid to rest.

In addition, we left a letter supposed to be written by Sweet to me, talking of our proposed route and saying that he agreed we had much better go towards Sivas, and giving a number of villages *en route*. This was supposed to be destroyed, and was to be found by accident by our orderly in a crumpled condition when and not until our escape was fully realized by the Turks. Our exit was to be made from a side door into an alley leading off the main street. This door was nailed up, but, like so many things in Turkey, it was done in a very slip-shod fashion with two boards having only two nails through each. To reach the door, entrance had to be obtained to a back garden, and this meant passing through another door which was padlocked every evening. Investigation proved that, though the padlock seemed sound, the staple might very easily be withdrawn and replaced afterwards. Six officers helped us enormously on the night we actually started. They were Major Corbett and Captain Raynor, 48th Pioneers, Captain R. Lowndes, R.G.A., Lieuts. Dooley, Cawley-Smith and Galloway, all I.A.R.O. Three opened the doors while another drowned their efforts by doing some violent bed repairing in a front room, this necessitating much hammering. The others kept a look-out on the sentries in the road or engaged them in amiable conversation in their best Turkish.

It had been difficult to decide which night to start. We had no tables giving the time the moon would rise and wanted to arrange to have a good hour of darkness after getting out. Finally we decided to start on Wednesday night, August 8th, at 10 p.m. Sweet, who lived in the other group of houses, arranged to come to dinner in our mess, being invited by Captain Martin, I.M.S., who not only assisted us in selecting our food but placed his room at our disposal for storing our kit and assembling in just before starting. Our plan was to wait behind the door in the alley until our mess cook, Prosser, should come and tap on the further side to show that all was clear. This man was in the habit of often going out after dark into the town disguised in an old coat, a fez, and a sham beard which he had himself made out of goat-skins.

His usual practice was to put the fez and beard on in the road and walk straight up past the sentries. On the night in question he got out in some such way and reconnoitred the route we should have to take to get out of the town on to the hill. Luckily we were on the edge of the town and a climb of two or three hundred yards through houses would take us out on to a Mohammedan graveyard on the hillside. As we were waiting silently in the dark behind the door, somebody gave a kerosine tin a kick, and the resulting clatter seemed bound to bring some one down upon us. However, nothing happened ; but a moment or two later we heard a heavy tread going slowly up the alley.

Our friends, watching, reported that this was the sergeant of the guard and we began to feel anxious. After another minute a tap came on the door. Our orderly had seen the sergeant safely into a small mosque round the corner, and everything was clear. We hurried out in single file, endeavouring to be quite silent but seeming to make an awful noise. I was wearing a pair of rope sole shoes and carrying my boots while the others had put old socks over their boots. In spite of our anything but noiseless departure we were not noticed. We scrambled up the hill and five

minutes later were under cover in the graveyard. Here we put our rucksacks and coats
on properly and prepared for an all-night trek.
In order to look less like officers and more
like local scallywags we had turned our coats
inside out and also carried our packs in a
blanket over one shoulder. We had decided
to wear old khaki, so as to be able to prove
we were really British if necessary in case of
accidents or bad luck. After taking us a little
further, our orderly friend shook hands with
us all round, and with a quiet word of farewell
and thanks for his invaluable assistance
we set off on our adventure.

We had to make a detour round the north of
the town across the main valley to get out to
the hills on the east. It was a clear, starry
night, but even so it was extraordinarily
difficult to recognize the hillsides which we
knew quite well by daylight. Hardly had
we gone a quarter of a mile before a dog began
to bark on the main road a little way off.
Later on, we did not pay much attention to
dogs, as we generally started at least one
every night by walking near a village or too
close to houses ; but this animal, being the
first and so near to the town, was anything
but pleasant to listen to. We scrambled
down a steep bank across a nullah and up a

gully running into a hill which we had to climb. The main nullah we had just crossed ran down towards the road passing the magazine, where by day there was always a guard. However, the dog soon ceased his complaint and quietness reigned. We were already beginning to feel the weights of our packs and, as the night was warm and our direction led up the stony, pathless side of a steep hill, we soon had to call a halt. In fact, although we did not admit it to each other, these moments were really almost the worst of our whole trip and each secretly thought what an idiot he had been ever to start. Having started, however, there was nothing for it but to continue and after a few minutes' rest we trudged on. A little further brought us out on the top, where we were annoyed to find that the moon was already well up, whereas we had reckoned on at least another half-hour of darkness.

During the last few days, we had carefully timed the moon's rising, and endeavoured to foretell the time for the night of our venture from comparisons with last year's almanac, which was all we had to go upon.

On the top of the hill, we could just make out the big square of the Turkish barracks lying down in the valley, a building which we

had passed almost every day during the last
year on our way to the football ground or on
walks.    Sweet wanted to give it a much wider
berth than I had intended, and in consequence
we were longer in getting down to the Ineboli
road which had to be crossed.    What was our
horror when we did approach it to hear the
creaking of country carts coming up towards
the town.    They seemed to be nearly opposite
to us and, as there was little cover and the
moon bright, the only thing to do was to lie
down in the ditch where we were and hope
the carts would pass.    We waited some time,
but yet more carts seemed to be approaching
and the drivers of others had halted almost
opposite to us.    There was nothing for it
but to turn back and try again lower down the
road.    After creeping back a little way on
all fours, we made a circle and came out
into an open field, heading once more for the
road.    Here we were dismayed to hear yet
another cart coming.    There was no cover
this time, not even a ditch, so we had to make
a dash for it.    This succeeded, and we were
across the road and some little distance into
a field of high crops on the far side before the
carts passed.    These carts were evidently
coming into the town for the following day's
market, but we had not counted on meeting

any at all.   We were now in the centre of the valley, and after crossing the stream made our way over some more fields to the Sinope road which we crossed without further adventure.

We had now reached open country, and after another half-mile rested again.   We were all feeling a bit done up and thought we had taken too much kit.   On starting again, we found that so far we were on the right track, but from now onwards we were going on a line we had not been on before even by day, and we regretted afterwards we had not for this first night kept straight on down the main Sinope road, along which we could have made good going, although it did not lead due east, which was the direction we had planned.   There were guard houses at intervals on this road, but I knew it for the first ten miles, having driven out with my colonel once when he was allowed a carriage to go fishing, this being a special favour which ceased to be granted as soon as the commandant of the town got to hear about it.

After several miles of up and down going, we reached the first river we had to cross. Along each side were irrigated maize-fields, but, fortunately, we managed to get through these and over the stream without coming to any houses or dogs, although there were villages and farms quite close. Another ascent met us on the further side and we plodded slowly on. The country was mostly open pasture and plough-land and there were few trees except those beside the streams in the valleys. Eventually, we got to the top of the ridge and a little later found ourselves overlooking another deep valley with a stream running a thousand feet below us. After a steep scramble down, we reached the water and called a halt. A tin of tongue presented by some one at the last minute was opened and eagerly consumed. It was now about 3 a.m. and we had not much more than another hour and a half to two hours before daylight, when we had to be safely under cover. On leaving the stream, we found we were not far from a hamlet, and roused the attentions of another dog. However, we plodded on once more. We could now see woods in the distance but, before reaching them, had some difficult country to cross. Tip and K. were feeling very done up and, as there were signs of dawn and other dogs taking up the hue and cry, we began to feel a bit anxious. These dogs seemed to be approaching from a village ; but we just managed to get away from them, although it seemed that they must rouse the whole countryside. During our next halt of a few minutes, we heard a cart coming along from the village, and, evidently, the peasants were already starting on the toil of another long harvest day, even though it was only just beginning to get light. Sweet and I had gone on, and on looking back could see no signs of the others. We went back a little way and luckily found them. We had just scrambled up a steep hill and were all fairly well done up. A little further took us to a pine wood, where we decided to lie up for the day. We lay just inside while the cart we had heard approached and passed on up the track we had just left. Then we turned and went into the wood, only to find, however, that sheep tracks ran everywhere and that the wood itself only extended two hundred yards to the top of the ridge where there were open fields—also, what was worse still, no part of the wood was really thick or offered good cover. Still, now it was too late to go on even if we had had the energy, and the only thing to do was to stay and make the best of it and trust to luck. We looked to each side, but the sheep-tracks were almost as thick in all directions. This meant that at any time, but particularly in the evening, we might expect a flock to come along and that would also mean a man or a boy and a dog.

It was, indeed, fortunate for our peace of mind during this first day that we did not know how soon our departure had been discovered. Actually, this was found out within two hours of our leaving, Sweet's absence being first ascertained by Sherif Bey, who simply snorted with rage and fury. What had happened was that our orderly was very nearly caught while trying to return to his quarters : he had to run for it, and in so doing lost one of his shoes. He got in safely, however, and had at once to destroy the other shoe. A few minutes later the Turkish guard came round, searching for the odd shoe, and listened carefully to the breathing and heart-beats of every orderly to see which one had been running. Luckily, however, our friend Prosser had had just long enough to compose himself in bed and was not detected.

# CHAPTER VII

## ON THE HILLS

WE made a breakfast from condensed milk and a small ration of biscuit and some cheese. We dared not make a fire, as people were working on the crops not very far away. After this we took it in turns to keep watch at the top edge of the wood. From this point a fine view could be had across the ridges back towards Kastamuni, although the town itself was hidden in the valley. One track was clearly visible and it was along this we expected to see signs of pursuit, if any; but there was nothing to be seen. The morning was perfect, and the country spread away in the sunshine back towards our old haunts. We appeared to have made at the very least ten miles from Kastamuni as the crow flies, but actually had marched much further owing to the detour round the town and our cross-country up and down route since. Towards the east more and higher hills could be seen, but we had to

MAP (SLIGHTLY REDUCED) USED ON JOURNEY TO BLACK SEA
(From Sir Henry Sykes "History of Persia")

be careful of reconnoitring, as there were flocks of sheep on the slopes not far away. All of us had sundry adjustments to make in our kit, which we felt we must lighten to enable us to make better going. My own costume consisted of an old and thin British warm over either a thin shirt or vest with old riding breeches and puttees. The others had regulation tunics, and Sweet was highly respectable, his uniform being nearly new. In the event of our posing as Germans we decided he must be the Herr Hauptmann, as in addition to his better clothes he knew more Turkish than the rest of us.

I set about a ruthless lightening of my coat by ripping out the lining, cutting off the turned-back cuffs and all other small portions that could be spared. We found it difficult to sleep, but felt good for another effort as soon as it began to get dark. About three o'clock, we relinquished our observation post, as all seemed quiet, and made another meal. Hardly had we finished before a dog appeared at the edge of the wood, and started barking as only Turkish dogs seem able to. A few moments later the expected boy also turned up and stared down upon us after quieting the dog. We thought this meant the village being roused at once, and deputed Sweet to go and spin a big yarn of some sort to the boy. He had scarcely got up before the boy vanished. The only thing to do now was to pack up and be off at once. This did not take long, as we had purposely remained ready to move at short notice. I abandoned in a bush my rope sole shoes which I had carried so far, and did not regret it, as they were some weight and very slippery to walk in. After creeping along, just inside the wood at the top of the slope, for a short distance, we found we were getting near a farm and could not go further before dark. We could not see the boy, but one or two sheep-dogs were visible not far off and matters did not look at all hopeful. However, no hue and cry followed, and very likely the boy had been as frightened of us as we of him, or he may have thought we were merely out from Kastamuni for a walk—although we had never been nearly so far before.

After waiting an hour at the edge of the wood, we saw the sheep approaching and knew they must be returning towards the farm. We got down the slope back into the wood and as much as possible off their line. There was a little more cover here, but still it was rather thin, and we could easily have been spotted by anyone looking for us. By and by the sheep trooped past, but no dog came near us and once more we breathed freely. To improve our prospects, it now began to cloud over and we had some rain. A dark cloudy night for cross-country tramping was anything but what we required; fortunately, it cleared later on, although even then it was black enough until the moon got up. Before starting again, the question of weight of kit had to be tackled and, although loath to part with any of our food, we decided to discard about two to three pounds each. For this sacrifice most of our cheese and meat was condemned. It seemed likely that the former would not remain good for very long, so that it was not much loss.

We decided to make a start before it got dark, and halt for food when we reached the river which we judged must run in the deep valley we were about to enter. Accordingly, we left the wood at 7.30 and set off across the corn-fields. A very steep and stony descent followed, and by the time we struck a road along the valley it was quite dark. We followed this road a short distance until we saw a light in a house a little way ahead. We then turned off and went straight down to the stream, where we proceeded to drink at length and then bathe. During this

K

bathe in the dark, I lost my soap, which was a great calamity, and Tip his knife. We dared not strike a light and had to be content to go on without. After a light meal, we went on up-stream. There appeared to be a ceremony of some sort going on at the house with a light, as there was a beating of drums. We crossed the stream a little higher up, taking off our boots and socks for the purpose. Luckily on the other bank we struck a track leading up the further side of the valley, which was very steep at this point. After climbing slowly up through brushwood in the dark for an hour, we came to more open country. Here there were farms, but we managed to avoid them successfully. The night had cleared sufficiently for us to see the stars, and we were steering a course about due east. A little further on, we got into a thick copse and had great difficulty in finding any track. Eventually, we emerged on to a road running along the ridge beyond which lay the next valley. After a short halt, we got under way once more and made a good distance down the road and along a path we found running down to the next valley.

We had to pass close through a farm and several houses, but luckily there were no dogs. After reaching the next stream and ascending it some way, we crossed over and found ourselves in a maize-field. We gathered some cobs, which were not yet ripe but would do to cook. A few yards further we saw a light in what appeared to be a sheep-pen. This we found was the usual custom in the country. All flocks are collected near the farm at night and a shepherd with a big resin torch sits up on guard. It was now just beginning to get light in the east, so we turned up the hill, and after a long and tiring climb found a tolerably safe hiding-place in a pine wood, Poor K. was very done up and the rest of us not much better, except Sweet, who, physically, was the toughest of us all. For nine hours we had been on the move, but we could not have done more than eight miles in a straight line—though at the time we thought it was much more. We lay down, and got two or three hours' sleep before preparing our next meal. We decided we would risk making a fire, and after hunting about for the most concealed spot boiled water in our canteens and made cocoa. This with a ration of biscuit formed our meal ; in addition, we used to allow ourselves a very small bit of chocolate and a little Horlick's milk. The latter by this time had coagulated into one sticky lump, necessitating hard work with the point of a knife before a fragment could be broken off.    Luckily, the fire burned without much smoke, and what little there was we endeavoured to mitigate by fanning it in different directions.    Not long after breakfast, we heard two horsemen trotting along a road through the wood and apparently quite close.    We thought they were probably gendarmes looking for us; but they passed on and did not pause to make investigations in our neighbourhood.    Another visitor also arrived, this being a man who was chopping wood, and worked round our knoll for some distance, but never came within sight.    Nothing further happened, and we spent a quiet day under the trees.    The weather was perfect, and had we had a little more to eat we should have enjoyed it immensely.    At five o'clock we made a stew of the maize with a little Oxo; and an hour later, after clearing up all traces of our activities, set off eastwards through the wood.

We soon reached the edge of the wood, and found ourselves looking southwards across a valley to a high range of hills.    On the lower slopes were several villages; but it was doubtful if people could see us, especially as our khaki was an excellent camouflage for this country: in fact, this had been a great recommendation to the proposal for marching in uniform. However, we endeavoured to keep out of sight ; and after travelling across the high ground for a mile reached a spot whence we could see the country eastwards and choose out our route for the coming night. The main valley had turned somewhat, and now ran eastwards through a rocky gorge which opened out beyond to a much greater width. This seemed to be our best line, and we thought there would surely be a track leading up the valley along the stream. At all events, our water was finished, and it was urgent to fill up our bottles again as soon as we could reach the river. We set off accordingly, but had not gone far before some one reported a man coming up the road ; we hid for some time, and when all was clear went on again, only to find we were descending to a field where women were still working, getting in the harvest. This necessitated another wait ; but as darkness was approaching the women soon left the field. In order to help out our scanty stock of food and make it go as far as possible, we were always on the look-out for any food we could pick up in the fields, and decided to take toll of this corn-field. The wheat was ripe and in a few minutes we all had a good pocketful, meaning to make a really substantial meal of wheat porridge next morning. By the time we reached a path near the bottom of the valley it was quite dark. This track seemed to lead downwards towards the river, and we followed it, expecting to get to the water any minute, but by and by it began to ascend again and then to get rougher and harder to find. This was very trying, as we all now wanted water badly, and so we finally decided to try a rocky gully leading steeply downwards. Sweet led the way, but, being too eager to get down, or through bad luck, slipped and hurt his leg in falling over a rock. It was very dark in the gully, and two candle ends which Sweet had brought proved invaluable. After climbing and crawling down some way over rocks, we were finally brought up by a sheer precipice falling 200 feet to the river. Tired and disgusted, we sat down to rest, and had to make up our minds to climb out the way we had come, and then either to go back down-stream or climb right to the top of the valley and advance and get down again higher up where the valley opened out. The latter course was adopted and, Tip giving us a good lead, we slowly and, in Sweet's case, painfully scrambled back. K. also had a bad time, as he was short-sighted and in such a dark spot it was no easy matter to get along.

# CHAPTER VIII

## SLOW PROGRESS

WE all felt dreadfully tired as well as thirsty. The past two nights had told on us; and without proper sleep and sufficient food we were not in the best trim for a third night of mountaineering. After getting back to the track, we had to climb up the side of the ravine, which was steep and rocky. Resting every few yards, we eventually reached the top and turned up-stream. The point where we had descended the gully must have been in almost the narrowest part of the gorge, and we could see that we should have to move some way along the crest before we could get down to the water. We were still ascending, and after continuing a little further decided to lie down till dawn, and then trust to getting down to the river and hiding before the country people were about. It was hopeless to try to get down again in the dark, even had we possessed the strength. Thirsty as we were, we got off to sleep; and, when

we woke, found it was already beginning to
get light. It had got much colder and our
thirst had accordingly diminished. I had
lost my cap the night before shortly before
we camped, and now luckily managed to
find it on going back a little way. We
pressed on and began to descend again. It
took us at least an hour down a very steep
tree-clad slope. The stones we set rolling
seemed to make a dreadful noise, but actually
must have been drowned in the roar of the
torrent below. As we neared the river, we
found we were quite close to a farm; but no
one was about, and we got down without
trouble. How we drank, and what a relief
it was to be beside water again! After a
wash, we set about getting a meal by preparing our wheat. It took some time to
get all the husks off the grain and longer to
boil it ; but it was very good and filling. Our
biscuits had numbered originally about thirty-
five each, so that as we had reckoned on a
journey of a fortnight to the coast we only
allowed ourselves two and a half per day.
We made cocoa, in addition to the porridge,
and went to sleep under the bushes, feeling
a great deal better than we had done for
some hours. Our camp was in a most ideal
spot. Below us, the river wound down

through the gorge, while the steep slopes on each side of the valley were covered with magnificent trees. There were a great many hazel nuts, but these were not yet ripe or we would have gathered a large number.

Later on, we produced our razor and, one by one, for the first time since leaving Kastamuni, made ourselves presentable. I got out the fishing line I had brought, but had no luck, chiefly owing to there being no worms to be seen in the soil on the river bank. The preserved meat seemed to have little attraction for the fish, of which there were plenty, and our biscuits were too precious to be used up in any way as bait.

We started off once more about 6.30, and after some rough going reached the wide part of the valley where fields came down to the river. Here we were soon brought to a stop by seeing people still at work. Retracing our steps, we crossed the stream and started to ascend the northern side of the valley, keeping roughly to our easterly direction. After a steep ascent, we reached a fair track, along which we made good progress. Once or twice we had to wait and hide owing to farm people being about ; but after it had got quite dark we got on again without interruption. On one occasion we passed close to a farm. There was a resin-wood torch burning in the yard, and just as we appeared a woman opened a window and looked out ; we expected her to see us, but possibly the glare from the torch was too strong, for she took no notice. By midnight, we had reached some high downland, where there seemed to be a large number of farms. After lying down for a couple of hours, we started off again ; but soon lost all sign of our track. Continuing in our direction with the help of the stars or compass, we suddenly found ourselves within range of some village dogs. These brutes devoted their attention to us long and loudly, and there was nothing for it but to get away across the fields as fast as we could. After a little time, we found a track which presently led into a pine wood. We trudged on through the trees for two hours, the track keeping on the crest of the hill and bending round gradually towards the north. This wood promised good cover for the next day, and as we seemed to have reached its edge we decided to stop here all day. We lay down until it grew light and then moved to the best spot we could find. This day was Sunday, August 12th, and we can only have achieved about 30 miles as the crow flies, although at the time we put it at 40.

Having picked no corn the night before, we had to be content with our small biscuit and meat ration which we carried, helped out with a fragment of Horlick and chocolate. Tip had not been feeling well all night and was now in considerable pain. He said porridge always laid him out, and our brew, which was not very well boiled, had proved no exception. As far as we could tell, it seemed to be appendicitis or something very like it. We discussed gloomy possibilities of giving ourselves up in the event of his not getting better ; but he remained determined to push on if he possibly could.

We reconnoitred our route for the coming night and set off again an hour before dusk. From the hill on which we had camped we could see a road leading in the direction we wanted, down a wide valley, and we determined to keep to this for some distance at all events. After forcing our way through brushwood to the foot of the hill, we were held up by hearing carts approaching and had to hide until they had gone past. We used this opportunity for a wash and to fill up our water-bottles from a small stream ; and then set off again, following the carts down the road. After marching for an hour we reached some corn stacks and collected more wheat. It took longer than when gathering it in an open field, but in half an hour we had accumulated enough, and again took the road. We had noticed that, further on, there seemed to be a good number of houses in the valley on our right which we should have to cross. Our direction now led down towards the river and the track passed through a stack yard. We were going quietly forward, when suddenly we were surprised by a number of dogs, which burst out upon us in full chorus from behind a stack. An old man appeared immediately afterwards and quieted the dogs, but luckily made no attempt to question us, and we passed on in silence. At night we always wore fezes and hoped thus to pass as Turks or Greeks.

A short distance further on, we crossed the stream and then were delighted to discover a maize-field, where we gathered a few of the biggest cobs we could find. A moment later some one discovered that beans and marrows were growing on the ground beneath the maize, so we helped ourselves to these also. The beans were of a dwarf French variety, which seems to be the most popular kind throughout the district. Thus provisioned, we set off up a wide valley leading up in front of us.

Poor Tip was having a hard time, and as we had to cross several ploughed fields before discovering any path, matters for him became much worse. He could manage to get along all right on a smooth path, but rough going gave him great pain. Fortunately, the road we now struck had quite a fair surface and we made a good pace for the next two hours, assisted by the moon. Finally, about 4 a.m., we lay down for an hour, until dawn, near the side of the road. We found we had over-slept ourselves on waking, as it was broad daylight ; so we had to hurry off up a small hill and hide in the bushes. The country round seemed more deserted in this part of the valley and we had got away from culti-vated land. As we were all now very done up, we decided to move down to the centre of the valley, which looked as if it must possess a stream. There we intended to hide for the rest of that day and the next. This we thought might give Tip a chance to get right again. After resting two or three hours on the hill, we scrambled down and eventually emerged in the main valley. Just before we reached it we as nearly as possible walked into two gendarmes, who were going up the valley road and crossed our path about a hundred yards ahead of us. However, they did not see us and all was still well. After crossing the main valley and stream, we found a small gully on the further side which seemed to offer us good cover, as well as having a small supply of water. As we crossed the river bed to reach it we came in view of a man and two boys working on an irrigation dam a little higher up. Luckily, they had their backs towards us and did not notice anything. A little way up the gully, we found a sheltered spot to camp in and prepared a meal, chiefly from the vegetables we had gathered the night before. We made Tip as comfortable as possible, and with the aid of hot compresses succeeded in making him feel easier. Nothing occurred during the day, and, after another stew had been consumed in the evening, we set about making ourselves comfortable for the night. With the aid of fir branches we made a tolerably soft couch. Tip, K. and I for purposes of additional warmth slept side by side under the most substantial part of the sail, while Sweet, who preferred to be on his own, rolled himself up in the lighter piece. We would have much enjoyed a little more warmth at nights and, in spite of putting on the few spare garments we each carried, we were always much too cold before morning.

Our plan now was to follow the road up to

the head of the valley and then steer as straight as possible for the Geuk Irmak valley, along which we knew ran the main road to Sinope. It was clear that we could not make fast enough progress at the present rate ever to reach Baffra before our provisions gave out ; our boots, also, were getting badly worn and much work was done in repairs at our various halts. Walking across rough country at night had damaged them much more severely than we had ever imagined could be the case.

The following day we spent in resting, cooking, and also shaving and washing. As one or two people had passed along the road in the afternoon, we did not like to make an early start and so waited until it was growing dark. For the first mile the track remained fairly good ; then it forked, and we chose the left-hand branch as leading in the direction we wanted most. It was now quite dark and the sky cloudy ; but what was much worse, the track got more and more indistinct as we slowly emerged into open country and fields at the head of the valley. Several times we had to halt and spread out to find the path ; and then, at last, when we did reach a cart track we almost walked right into a big farm. After pausing to reconnoitre, we decided to try to skirt it on the left, and had got half way round when a sheep-dog heard us and started off at full blast. There was a shepherd sitting with a torch in one of the farm buildings, but he took no notice. Shortly afterwards we found a field of beans to which we helped ourselves, and then had to make a diversion to avoid another house. This led us into a pinewood and we were soon forced to give it up until morning, as we could see no way through in the darkness. We lay down close together and got a few hours' sleep before the first sign of daylight roused us to continue our journey. We had to pass closer than we liked to a farm ; but no one was about yet and we got away on to a high ridge covered with brushwood. After making our way for a short time along this, we halted and made cocoa, which with a biscuit formed our breakfast. By this time our biscuits had broken up into small fragments, so that we had to estimate how many bits were equal to a whole biscuit. Our experiences of the night before forced us to the conclusion that it was hopeless trying to do a good march by night unless on a good track ; and we, therefore, decided to cut across a low cultivated stretch of land to the forest covering the opposite ridge and continue by daylight until reaching

the Geuk Irmak. It was now about nine
o'clock and the peasants were at work in the
fields almost all round us.   There was no safe
way of reaching the woods opposite without
exposing ourselves to view, and the only
thing was to do the best we could and use all
the cover available.   On getting down to a
stream from a steep hill, we found we were close
to some women and children.   The latter saw
us, but the women were too busy to notice
us and we reached cover in a nullah on the
further side without any alarm being raised.
Our next encounter was with an old Turk.
He saw us just before we saw him and was off
to ground in some cover before one could say
knife.   Evidently, he was very much more
startled at seeing us than we were at seeing
him.   After this we were not seen by any
other people, and after skirting a harvest
field got well into the forest.   At two o'clock
we halted, and having slept for two hours
made another stew and prepared to go on
till dark.   We were in a big forest chiefly of
huge pines which were being cut in places for
resin.   Our direction was now nearly due
north, and every rise we topped would, we
hoped, bring us in view of the Geuk Irmak
valley.   As is generally the case, the
longed-for view was very slow in making its

appearance, and we had to bivouac for the night without reaching our goal. We had passed a small flour mill, driven by a water wheel. Sweet had investigated it for flour, but it was swept and garnished and absolutely empty.

# CHAPTER IX

NEXT morning we were off at the first streak of dawn, after a very cold night. We were in a narrow valley, and look where we would we could not find the track we had seen not long before halting the previous night. The hills were too steep and wooded to make it possible to get along low down by the stream, so there was no other course open except to start climbing again in the hope of meeting the track at a higher level. This we succeeded in doing after toiling up some distance. Following the track, we emerged after a couple of miles on a hill overlooking the long expected Geuk Irmak. It was too late in the morning and the neighbourhood too populous to make further progress possible, so we bivouacked close by in the wood and hoped to make good distance that night along the main road in the valley. Starting an hour before dark, we were forced to wait for a home-coming couple who were slowly returning along the track we were intending to take. When they were safely off the scene, we had to scramble down through the thickest copse it was ever our misfortune to meet with, and by the time we had reached the river it was quite dark. As on all such occasions, we took off our boots and socks to cross and replaced them on the other side, only to find soon after that there was another branch of the river which we had not been able to see in the dark, so that the process had to be repeated. Even then we were not over dry-shod, as there were now several irrigated fields to be crossed before we could get to the road. Creeping along the small bund dividing two fields, we endeavoured to keep on dry ground ; but were not very successful. Finally, we reached a big irrigation nullah, which meant another wade. We were now, at last, on the main road ; but it had taken us two hours' hard going to get there, which was a great disappointment. Soon after starting again, we met a couple of men on ponies, driving cattle. At the time we were rather separated ; Tip and I escaped observation, but Sweet and K. were not so lucky, for the men stopped and asked who they were. Sweet promptly said " Germans " and gave a few details. The men, however, declared they were prisoners, but did not seem disposed to make trouble, and moved on again after a few minutes, much to Sweet's relief.

After another hour's trek, we felt too exhausted to go further, and lay down, intending to do a little more at dawn. The mosquitoes were a great pest in this valley and we had a very poor night's sleep. We had now come down to a much lower elevation : Kastamuni was 2,500 feet above sea, but this spot could scarcely be 1,000 feet. As soon as it grew light in the morning we were off again along the road, after filling up our water-bottles from the river and investigating another flour mill which proved to be empty. Very soon we came to a picturesque old wooden bridge spanning the stream and, after crossing this, decided to lie up for the day on the hill-side above. The valley became wider at this point and several hamlets and farms were to be seen ; it therefore behoved us to get under cover as quickly as possible, since the peasants are very early astir. We found a good place and lit a fire. This was, perhaps, rather rash, but we felt that it was worth risking a good deal to have something hot to drink. As we had had no luck in getting vegetables the night before, we had to be content with small rations. After an uneventful sunny day, we moved down to the road in the evening, and after filling our bottles with water from the river gathered some maize and marrows from a field close by. We then set off down the road and made very fair progress for the next three hours.

Loaded as we were with several extra pounds each of marrow, we got more tired than would otherwise have been the case. Eventually, the road led us into a village, and we had to walk straight past some people coming towards us. They took no notice, however, and we went on. A little further, there was a light in a flour mill, which was grinding away as hard as it could go, being driven by a small water turbine. There seemed to be no track by which we could avoid going right through the village, and after retracing our steps once or twice we decided there was nothing else for it. We tramped down the road past several old fellows who were sitting outside a house and were probably interested in the activities of the flour mill. Most likely, by grinding secretly at night, it is possible to escape the Government's taxes on flour, but needless to say we did not stop to make inquiries. The road seemed to take us nowhere. After visiting one or two back yards and coming out in another place on top of a house, we had eventually to retrace our steps past the old men to the end of the village which we had first entered. How that road made its way out we never discovered and, in consequence, lost a good deal of time and distance.

After sleeping for a couple of hours in a graveyard, we set off with the first streak of dawn to make a circuit round the south side of the village, and reached a hill which promised safety for the day. It took us a long time and many halts had to be made. We disposed of our marrows by eating them raw, and decided that they were too heavy to be worth carrying any distance in future. Finally, we reached a snug spot in brushwood high up on the hill and made ourselves as comfortable as circumstances would allow.

In the afternoon, I decided to go to the top of the hill to try to locate our exact position in the valley. After a steep climb I got a splendid view all round and discovered a convenient track for us to follow as soon as it grew dark. A town was clearly visible a few miles further on, and this I felt sure must be Duraghan, although the road leading to it did not correspond with what was shown on our map. However, we decided that it must be this place, as by our calculations we reckoned we must have come every bit of the distance. Our disgust may be imagined when on the following day we found the place was really Boiabad, a town 30 miles short of Duraghan.

Just after getting back to our bivouac, it came on to pour, but luckily we managed to get a fire going and a stew made just in time. However, the result was that we started marching an hour later, soaked very nearly to the skin, and with no prospect of being able to get dry in the near future. We came close to the town, as it was getting dark, and after crossing a stream had some discussion as to which road to take. Finally, we selected a track which we thought must lead into the main valley, where we were certain the main road would run on our side of the river. As a matter of fact, it had crossed to the other side and we did not meet it till next day. We continued along this track till midnight, when we lay down for a little sleep ; but it was too cold to be possible in our wet things and in an hour we were up and off again. A few miles further on, we found we were close to a village through which the track ran and, joyful sight, there were several corn stacks close by. These promised a warm shelter until dawn ; but it was not to be. The usual village dog had already heard us and although we remained stock still he would not cease his frantic barking. One old peasant had already been roused up and came slowly towards us. Our only course was to go straight on ; and we went right into the village, past several houses, through a cow pen, over a hedge and so on to the moor beyond. Just as we got clear some sportsmen let off a shot-gun. No pellets came near us and it was probably only meant as a warning to robbers !

Luckily, we were not followed and got away over the hill, steering east. After some distance we rested again, until morning should show us our whereabouts. We were evidently some way from the river and a good height up. As it began to get light, we moved off towards the river, hoping to find a snug hiding-place near the water. No such luck was in store for us, for just as we reached a slope overlooking the river we saw a small village at our feet, and the village dogs saw us almost at the same moment. Wearily we retraced our steps uphill, and when out of range of the dogs held a council as to our future efforts. It was clear that while walking by night we were covering very little distance, and that at this rate the food we carried would be exhausted long before we reached the sea. We decided, therefore, that our only hope lay in bluffing the country people that we were Germans and buying food where we could. Accordingly, we made for the first house we could see, where a miserable peasant and two women were working. We explained that we were Germans surveying, and produced our maps and passport in support of this contention. They did not doubt us ; but they had no food to sell and, indeed, looked as poor and wretched as people well could. However, they referred us to their master, who was the headman of the locality. We crossed a few fields and were then met by this gentleman, to whom we told the same story. He led us into his house and providing us with seats gave orders for food to be prepared. In the meanwhile, Sweet carried on a conversation to the best of his ability. It appeared that our host was one Ahmed Chaoush (sergeant) who had been fighting against us in Gallipoli but now had a year's sick leave. He took in our story, but asked some awkward questions, such as why we carried no revolvers ? Sweet had to pretend not to understand and, luckily, Ahmed did not become suspicious. We gathered from him that the town we had passed in the night was Boiabad and that Duraghan was several hours' distance in front of us. This was a cruel blow, and only showed us how much slower we had been than we thought. In the meantime, the chaoush had produced some small pears which were soon disposed of. Finally, after much anxious speculation as to whether or no our host intended to give us a meal, real signs of preparation appeared for that eagerly expected event.

A few minutes later a small circular table was produced and several dishes were brought in. These consisted of cucumber sliced up in milk, small wads of boiled flour in milk, yoghourt or curdled milk and chapatties— a feast such as we had hardly dared to hope for. Turkish fashion, we sat round, each armed with a wooden spoon and dipped in the same dish, emptying one after another. It is etiquette on such occasions to wait until the next man has taken a spoonful so that all may get the same number in the end, but I fear we were not always so scrupulous and ate as fast as our usual habits would allow. When the table and dishes had been cleared away, Ahmed was given a little English tobacco and told it was the best German variety. Soon after we bid him a grateful farewell, and, although he was unwilling to take anything, succeeded in getting him to accept some money. We felt that to accept his hospitality and humbug him without any payment would scarcely be playing the game. He directed us towards our road, for which we had to descend again to the main valley and cross the river. On the further side we were delayed by a large irrigation nullah. When across this we found a good many blackberries and some onions in a field. The latter we seized upon with avidity, as being the first we had met with. There was some doubt as to which of two roads we should take, but it was decided to pursue one which some women had pointed out as the right road to Duraghan. This led straight away from the river and began to climb steeply. After a couple of hours, we had ascended some distance and decided to bivouac till the afternoon. The sun was pretty hot, but we were now high up and on top of a small hill from which the surrounding ranges could be clearly seen. It was evident that we had not come in the direction we had intended, but, on the other hand, we were now heading direct for the sea. After some discussion and poring over the map, we decided that our only real chance of reaching the sea lay in making a bee-line across country as nearly as possible in a north-easterly direction, buying food where we could and walking by day.   If we had gone on we should not only have had to skirt Duraghan by night, or make a big detour by day, but the distance down to the sea would have been very much greater.   In addition, it would have been much hotter for walking, with the extra hardship of mosquitoes at night.

# CHAPTER X

## REACHING THE COAST

WE made it to be 30 miles in a straight line to the sea from the spot where we now lay and hoped to do the distance in three days. After the chaoush's hospitality at breakfast we scarcely felt inclined for another meal till the afternoon, when we made tea, and then packed up, intending to follow up a track beside a stream which flowed down from the range we had now determined to cross. Descending our hill, we came to a small village, and thought it would be just as well to see if we could purchase any provisions before going further. We asked some children for eggs, whereupon a Turkish matron of an unusually agreeable type came out and after a little parleying brought us quite a royal supper. This consisted mainly of an excellent tomato stew, chapatties, yoghourt and fruit. Taking into account what we had accumulated from Ahmed Chaoush, we had now got quite a good stock of chapatties.   The amusement afforded by bluffing these good people had considerably raised our spirits, but all at once the good dame serving us staggered us completely by saying casually she had seen us in Kastamuni.   We assured her it must have been other people, as we had no connection with Kastamuni and were real Germans from Angora.

Just before leaving a man appeared who eyed us very suspiciously, and we were glad to get away without waiting to make his acquaintance.   We had hardly gone a mile before an old man ran to meet us with his cap full of apples.   We seemed almost to be entering on a triumphal progress and were tremendously amused.   Several houses and a large village were passed without event, but a little further on we found several men with mules resting a short distance from the road.   They called to us, and probably wanted to continue their journey in our company, but it was sailing nearer the wind than we cared for and, pretending we had to go on at once, we did not stop to hear anything more from them.   Just before dark we passed through a very picturesque gorge, where the stream ran through a deep narrow gateway between two enormous masses of rock, and beyond this found a nook to sleep in for the night where we should be protected from the wind. This had been a truly great day, and its success seemed to confirm the wisdom of our new policy.

Early the following morning, we were once more pursuing our path, which now became fainter and steeper as it rose towards the rocky ridge towering above us. Towards eleven o'clock, we reached some poor houses not far below the crest. Hoping to be able to purchase food, we stopped and made inquiries, but all the chief people seemed to be away at some market and there was nothing to be had. We continued on our way and after another hour's tramp came to a cattle trough by the side of the path. As there was water flowing here, we decided to halt till the afternoon, and found a snug spot a few yards up the hill. In the afternoon, after washing and shaving, we were nearly discovered by a man who appeared to be a gendarme. He came riding down the path and stopped to water his horse at the trough, but passed on without noticing anything. Soon afterwards we were again marching, still upwards towards the crest of the mountain ridge. We must have been now over 4,000 feet up, and hoped when we reached the top we should actually see the sea. An hour's trek took us to a poor village standing very high and, probably, in winter almost always in the clouds. An ill-clad woman informed us that she was a Greek who had only just arrived from Kastamuni. She seemed to have a pretty clear notion as to what we really were, but said nothing and, eventually, got us yoghourt and some chapatties. Our direction was now about north-east and we were making for Tel Kelik, a small place marked on the map, a little on the northern side of the watershed. Most of the peasants seemed never to have heard of it, and we had some difficulty in getting on to a path leading in the right direction. As it grew dusk, we found ourselves in a second village at almost the same elevation ; there was no one about, but eventually a man turned up who said he was on his way home to another village. The village women in particular were most suspicious, declaring that there was no food anywhere ; and it was not until some little while later, when the colour of our money had been clearly shown, that anything was forthcoming. We had intended to spend the night in a village hut if possible, as the only alternative was sleeping in the mist, which at 4,000 feet was a cold and dreary prospect.

M

However, after some parleying, we were led
to what proved to be the travellers' rest hut.
Our story was absorbed with due interest, a
large fire lighted and some food brought in.
We lay down on mats on the floor, rejoicing
in the warmth and, if undisturbed by smaller
visitors, felt we should have a really good
night's rest.  Several village worthies looked
in during the evening to see the Almans
(Germans) and we hope were not disappointed.
A young soldier just returned on leave from
Constantinople helped to procure some butter
and syrup for us.  The latter is a poor substitute for treacle and seems to be made from
raisins.  This reception in a travellers' rest
hut was the limit reached by our bluff ; it gave
us much satisfaction to think how annoyed
our Turkish friends in Kastamuni would be
to know of our being entertained in such a
manner.

We had a splendid night, although lying
on the floor, and in the morning obtained a
little more food and some butter through our
soldier friend.  After a hasty meal we hurried
off with our first acquaintance of the previous
night as guide to put us on the right road.  We
were soon at the highest point of the range,
although as yet the sea was not in view.  A
little further on, after having bought a large

knife from our friend, we bade him good-bye with many expressions of gratitude. Tel Kelik was now quite close, and it was fortunate that we were not compelled to march through it, since we found later that there was a Turkish detachment stationed in the village. Leaving the Tel Kelik valley, we climbed the hill on our side and an hour later—at 9.30—were delighted at finding the sea stretching out before us in the sunshine. It looked about fifteen miles off, but the mere sight seemed to raise our spirits marvellously, and we were, perhaps, almost as elated as Xenophon's men when the same sea greeted their gaze at Trebizond. We were now in a copse and decided to halt till evening. To celebrate the occasion, we made a late breakfast of buttered eggs, the eggs having been bought at a cottage we had passed during the morning. The next work in front of us was to make something of the coarse flour which we had procured two days previously from the Greek woman. Sweet got to work and, using some of the butter and our last tin of condensed milk, turned out a very fine dough. Baking was the chief difficulty and, after trying to make an oven, in the end we had to be content with making small chapatties on our diminutive frying-pan turned upside down and on the lid of a canteen. The results were very satisfactory, although consisting largely of fragments.

At four o'clock in the afternoon, we set off again and by dark had gone a good distance, and, after finding a sheltered spot for the night, collected a quantity of dead bracken to make ourselves as comfortable as possible.

We were off again early next morning, and had a steep scramble down through a wood, and eventually, to a stream at the bottom of a deep valley. Here there were a number of blackberries which we took advantage of, and then climbed the further side, coming out at last on the top and finding nothing now lay between ourselves and the beach, which must have been only three miles away at the nearest point. A moment later a sailing boat was seen close in to the shore and two or three others soon after. We were overjoyed at this, as it meant that boats were still being used along the coast and that there was no truth in all the stories we had heard in Kastamuni to the effect that no boats were now plying. There was a small wooded hill projecting into the sea a little west of where we now were, and from its summit there would be a good view of the coast in each direction ; on the other hand we knew we could not be far from

the town of Jerse, and going west **meant**
getting still nearer to it.   Also, there were
several farms and open country between us
and the hill, and we were now very anxious
not to be seen at all if we could help it.   In
the end, we decided to stay where we were
for the day and go straight down to the
shore in front of us late in the afternoon.
The wood we were in was very thick and, try
as we might, no good spot for a halt could
be found which would also give us a clear
outlook on to the coast and any boats sailing
along it.   We had to be content to do without further observation of the sailing boats,
and bivouacked amongst the trees.   **Tea**
was made and a frugal meal of biscuits
followed : our cocoa was now all exhausted,
and greatly did we wish we had brought more
of it in the place of some other things.

# CHAPTER XI

IN the afternoon, we sewed together the two halves of the sail and cut a handle for our axe head so as to be as ready as possible in the event of discovering a boat. After making a stew from some beans we had gathered in a field on the hill that morning, we packed up and set off, full of hope and excitement. The question of going across to the wooded hill arose again when we got clear of the wood, but it was thrown out, and, bitterly did we regret it next day. Turning down to the shore, we crossed the road and, eventually, reached the beach just as it was getting dark. There were one or two small houses just on our right above the shingle, and we were reconnoitring carefully when a big rowing boat was seen coming along close to the beach, rowed by some eight men. It went a quarter of a mile further along, and the boat was then pulled up by the men and others who appeared from the houses. It was too dark to see what they were, but for some unknown reason we did not suspect that they were men of a guard at this place, or connect the houses with a place shown on one of our maps as being somewhere near here. We debated whether to go along the coast when it was quite dark and reconnoitre, or whether to wait for dawn. In any case, it seemed hopeless to think we could push off the boat which had just been pulled up : it was far too heavy and they had brought it up a long way. Finally, we decided to wait till dawn and then go along and see what we could find.

As soon as it began to get light next morning, August 23rd, we were up ; our excitement was increased by seeing a small boat moored a little way from the beach. This had mast and sail and was just the size of boat we were hoping for. We crept quietly down to a track along the shingle. Sweet was in front and reported seeing a peasant near the first house. We walked quickly on finding that there were rather more tumble-down houses than we had expected. However, it was too early for people to be about and there seemed no reason to suspect danger. We were hurrying on towards the boat we had seen, when we passed the end of a tumble-down boat-house and, to our dismay, found a

Turkish sentry standing just inside. He stopped Sweet, while we three hurried on a little further. Sweet told him we were Germans bound for Samsun, the next port along the coast. However, the old man insisted on telling his chaoush or sergeant. Meanwhile Sweet had rejoined us, but there was no chance of getting away, as by this time three or four others of the guard had turned out. The sergeant had us brought back to the guard-house, where the next scene of the pantomime began. Sweet, as had been previously arranged, was to play the part of a German officer, while we three were orderlies. Accordingly, we carried his pack for him, jumped up and down and saluted and, generally, behaved in a manner calculated to show our subservience. Meanwhile, the chaoush who was in charge of the guard at this place— a village called Kusafet—was evidently not at all sure of his ground, and suggested we should go with him to Jerse. We replied we were going in the opposite direction, and wanted a boat with which to reach Samsun. The boat which had been moored off the beach had now been brought to shore and was landing some stores for the guard. We spoke to the skipper of this boat and, finding he came from Trebizond and knew a little

English, hoped he would be amenable to helping us. Our idea was that having got on board for Samsun we could persuade him for a consideration to take us on to Trebizond, which was in Russian hands.

He went upstairs to confer with the chaoush, but whether he gave us away or not we were never quite sure. He came down advising us to go to Jerse and see the commandant there. This man, he assured us, knew no English or German, and was very ignorant and would believe our story. The chaoush wanted to make us march to Jerse, but we refused and, eventually, set off in the boat under the escort of the chaoush and two other armed soldiers. Before leaving we had obtained some chapatties, and a little raw fish which was better eating than we had expected. On the way we suggested to the skipper that with the help of the crew we could easily overpower the guard and then set sail east ; but he would not agree, and with the probability of the crew of five joining the guard we should have stood no chance at all. Hugging the coast, we reached Jerse in two hours, finding a small Turkish town built on a slight promontory. On the way, we passed the wooded hill we had talked about so often the day before. We should have been quite safe on this hill and, what was more, should have seen two or three boats in which we could probably have got away without much trouble. On reaching Jerse we found ourselves moored beside a small patrol boat of the Turkish navy, one of the crew of which said openly we were English. However, Sweet had gone ashore with the chaoush, and we were left hoping for the best, but fearing the game was up. Half an hour later we were summoned to join Sweet, and were conducted with him to a police station. Here Tip was made to speak on the 'phone to a German officer at Sinope. He could think of nothing to say but " Sprechen sie Deutsch," to which the Teuton eagerly responded at the other end. After shouting this down the 'phone several times Tip threw down the receiver, declaring it was out of order ! Another man coming into the station declared he had seen two of us at Kastamuni. We were then taken to the commandant of the town and agreed it was useless to try to bluff any longer, since they believed us to be English spies and it was only a matter of getting hold of any German for our whole story to fall to the ground. We, therefore, admitted that we had escaped from Kastamuni, saying we had been so long prisoners that we wanted to get home. The commandant was one of the best types of Turkish officer it had been our fortune to meet and was most polite. We were searched, and our maps and compasses and diaries taken, except from K., who managed to smuggle his map through. My original compass, not being recognized as such, was not taken.

Sweet told us that on first landing he had seen the commandant of the local *gendarmerie*, whom he had no difficulty in bluffing, as the skipper had foretold. Sweet told him we were on our way to the Caucasus to help in preparing a coming offensive for the Turks. He took all this in and Sweet was congratulating himself that our troubles were over. After giving Sweet coffee he said, no doubt, we would now like to be going on our way to Samsun. Sweet agreed, and they were just coming back to rejoin us when the Yuzbashi mentioned that there was a colonel who was commandant of the town and that he would probably like to see Sweet before he left. The fat was then in the fire. Sweet proffered our passport, but the colonel was suspicious and a Turkish naval officer whom he called in confirmed his ideas that we were British. The colonel told us later that there were two mistakes in our passport, which otherwise he evidently thought was quite good. He had our names and had been warned of our escape some two or three days after we had left Kastamuni.

The yuzbashi, finding how thoroughly he had been bluffed, was now equally frantic in his wrath. We were said to be going off that day to Sinope, and he was already preparing to handcuff us together in pairs. Luckily, the colonel turned up in time to prevent this. Most of our money was now taken and a receipt given to us for it. A little later we were told we were not going that day and were given a better room in the police station. The chaoush was very pleased with himself and told us he was going to accompany us to Kastamuni. He, also, it appeared, had been warned of our escape and, having passed through Kastamuni recently, probably suspected us more quickly than he would otherwise have done. The colonel came in to see us, and endeavoured to find out as much as he could from us as to which way we had come and how we had got food, but we told him very little. We got some food sent in and finally lay down on the floor for the night. Tip was now suffering again from his previous complaint, and we insisted that a doctor should be brought. However, no one was forthcoming. Next

morning we were allowed to go into the bazaar
to buy a few things needful, and on our return
were told to get ready to march at once. A
small donkey was brought up and on this we
loaded our kit.

Tip was still feeling very poorly and had
a bad time on the march. After some
eight miles, mostly along by the sea, we
reached some Turkish barracks which had
evidently been only recently put up. They
were wooden buildings, but, fortunately,
cleaner than might have been expected. We
were put into a small corner room in the
officers' quarters and were much amused to
find that no less than three sentries were
posted to guard us ; one outside the door,
and one outside each window.

The officers consisted of a fat and surly
yuzbashi and an Arab lieutenant, a huge man
who was most genial and friendly. He told
us his home was near Mosul, but he refused
to believe that the British were in Bagdad and
evidently thought we were trying to bluff
him, the ignorance pervading all classes in
Turkey as to what is happening in the outside world being colossal.

# CHAPTER XII

WE had several visits from the Arab officers, and they very kindly gave us a share of their food, which consisted chiefly of a vegetable stew. The following morning we were given a bread ration for five days and told to get ready at once. Tip was not fit to move, but they would not listen to us and dragged him out. We found a small pony had been brought, so Tip mounted this and we set off with a guard of a sergeant and eight privates; our former friend, the chaoush from Kusafet, was not coming with us after all and in his place we had a truculent quick-tempered fellow who looked as if he would be anything but an agreeable companion on the march. The men were evidently in the best of spirits, a visit to Kastamuni being a great event for them. In addition, they carried a good deal of tobacco, which they doubtless expected to sell again at a large profit on arrival. A great deal of tobacco is grown in the coast districts, more particularly near Samsun. We set off at a very easy pace and after passing the German wireless station soon had a halt. The guard had two donkeys which carried their kit, but the chaoush would not hear of us putting our packs on them as well. After another halt in a village, we reached a caravanserai early in the afternoon, where the guard prepared their food, the man who owned the donkeys acting as cook to the chaoush. This fellow had not even the disreputable uniform which the average Turkish soldier possesses, but was clothed in thin black stuff. His efforts produced boiled rice over which a little melted butter was poured. This was taken to a raised corner where he and the chaoush proceeded to shovel it into their mouths from the same bowl, etiquette prescribing that the two parties should take spoonfuls strictly in turn. An hour later we were off again, and began to ascend the lower slopes of the mountains we had crossed a few days previously. Now, however, we were on the so-called main road. It was one of the worst roads it had been our lot ever to have seen, and we were truly thankful we were not travelling in carts. Long stretches were strewn with blocks of stone, which had been, apparently, left there promiscuously by some contractor who had not finished his job, like so many others in this country. An hour or two later, after ascending some little distance, we stopped for the chaoush to get his pony shod. This animal he had commandeered at a village we had passed through, and now fancied himself to no small extent as a mounted man. After a long wait the shoeing was at last accomplished and we set off once more. To our delight the chaoush had also procured a second pony, and on this we were allowed to load our packs. About eight o'clock we reached a small village, where we were to spend the night ; an empty log hut was found and a fire made in the large open hearth. We were given one side of the chief room while most of the guard slept on the rest of the floor. With some eggs we had bought we made a very good supper and, thanks to the fire, were as comfortable as the circumstances would allow. We were now high up and it would have been very cold to bivouac in the open, as we must have been surrounded by clouds during the night. Before going off to sleep we considered the chances of escape. There would be little chance after another day or two when we had got further from the sea and were halting in larger villages, so that the present night seemed the only practical time, should opportunity offer. However, we soon came to the conclusion that it was quite impossible, as not only was there a sentry in the narrow passage outside the door but one or two of the askars in our room were told to keep awake in turns. The only exit was the door, to reach which we should have to walk over several of our guard.

First thing in the morning, August 27th, we were off again up the road. It was a glorious day and nothing happened beyond the usual halts every hour or so. We discussed our escapade once more, again deciding we had had a good run for our money, but that we had not been cautious enough when we did reach the coast. We went over afresh the various routes possible and alterations in plans which we would have adopted with the experience now gained. It was about nine o'clock and we had been on the march fully two hours when suddenly with a cry of " Askar " shots rang out from the near side of the road. For a moment we were too startled to know what to make of it. Then K. and I made a dive down the " khud " side, as the open road seemed anything but the best place to stay in. The first shot had

N

bowled over the man in black who was riding a donkey in front. We had been told so much at Kastamuni about the bandits infesting the hills that we quite thought we might have fallen amongst a party of them and that to be taken and held to ransom would be a worse fate than returning for a few months to the civil prison at Kastamuni or Angora.

On going a little way down the hill I saw a man whom I at first thought to be the chaoush, but as he beckoned to me saying " Venez, venez," I saw that this was one of the new arrivals. He wanted me to go off down the hill with him, but after descending a little way I explained there were other officers on the road and I must go back to them. In the meantime, he was very voluble and excited, but I could not gather who they were or what had brought them. On arriving back on the road I found K. and Tip ; the fighting was now over, and three of the brigands were collecting the askars' rifles and ammunition. The guard had put up no show at all and the nine of them were all disarmed and standing like sheep within two minutes, thanks almost entirely to the efforts of the three now collecting their arms, since my friend had been too far down the bank to have done much firing himself. The

question now was whether we were to go with
these fellows. K. was all for going off at
once, but Tip and I hesitated as to the position we should be in, if caught again by the
Turks before getting away. Our new friends
would, of course, have been shot as outlaws,
and we should very likely have shared the
same fate. We took them aside and at length
made out that they were adherents of the old
Turk party and had no use whatever for
Enver and his Government. They said they
had come specially to rescue us, and had a
boat ready to put off for either Trebizond
of Sevastopol in three or four days' time.
After realizing this, a process which took
some time, as our knowledge of the language
was very sketchy, we decided to throw in our
fortunes with our new friends, as it seemed a
heaven-sent chance of getting out of the
country and almost too good to be true.
We had seen nothing of Sweet since the firing
started and now began to shout for him and
search on each side of the road. Our new
friends set the old guard on to look for him,
but not a sign of him could we see and no
response came to our calls. After searching
and shouting for an hour, we finally had to
give it up, and leaving the guard in the road
set off with our new acquaintances, whom we

will now style the "akhardash"—or comrades —as that was the name they always used for themselves and their supporters. As far as we could see, Sweet must have dashed away when the first shots rang out, thinking no doubt that this was a splendid opportunity of getting free again. It was very hard luck for him, especially as he had all along been one of the keenest and most energetic of the party. The old guard watched us go without emotion; they were apparently used to surprises of this sort. The chaoush remarked that we should now go to our homes, and we often wondered what happened to him when he got back to the barracks and reported.

He would be sure to say his party had been greatly outnumbered and were only disarmed after a prolonged resistance, but, nevertheless, he was probably reduced to a private. Besides the man in black who had been killed, two of the others had been wounded. Considering the rate at which the akhardash started firing, at a range of only twenty yards or so, the wonder is they did not hit many more; probably after inflicting a few casualties to start with they afterwards fired high on purpose. The guard, beyond firing one or two shots, seemed to have made no resistance at all. They were completely surprised

MAP (REDUCED) SHOWING ROUTE OF ESCAPE

and totally unready for such an occurrence.
Tip had an unenviable experience. He was
riding his pony when the shooting began and
had our rucksacks festooned round his saddle
and over his legs so that he could not dismount
in a hurry and found himself in a helpless
position in a small storm of bullets. Finally,
he was dragged to the ground by the tallest
of the akhardash, who proceeded to kiss him
with much fervour ! This man, whose name
was Musa, became our great friend. He was
a tall lithe fellow and was always ready to
do everything he possibly could for our comfort during the following weeks. The leader,
whom we always rather suspected of having
played the part of the Duke of Plaza Toro in
the actual scrap, was one Bihgar Bey, a most
evil-looking gentleman. In fact none of the
four at the time we first saw them presented
an appearance likely to inspire any confidence,
but resembled more the types one sees por-
trayed as those of the greatest criminals.
Bihgar Bey, we learnt later, was one of a
dozen implicated in the murder of Mahomed
Shevket Pasha[1] some years previously, but
as he alone when caught was not in possession
of arms his sentence was only one of transporta-
tion, while all the others were put to death.

---

[1] Grand Vizier, 1913.

The other two were Keor, an old Armenian who looked as if he had led a very hard life, and Kiarmil, a little man who had been a sergeant-major in the Turkish forces during the late Balkan war. Their looks, however, entirely belied them, as will be seen from our subsequent experiences, when on all occasions they went out of their way to lessen the hardships of our life in the woods. During the following days we found that they had been able to pay a certain sum yearly to avoid military service up to a few months previously, when all such privileges had been cancelled. They had then been forced either to serve or become outlaws, and had chosen the latter alternative. After living in the woods supported by more law-abiding friends, of whom they seemed to have a great number dotted about the country, they had decided to leave for Russia, and made arrangements with a man in Sinope to embark in his boat when all their party had been gathered and all arrangements completed. In the meantime, a gendarme at Sinope, who was also of their political views, had given them news of our recapture and march back to Kastamuni. They determined thereupon to effect our rescue, and the evening before had made a forced march of over twenty miles. At first, we could not understand why they had taken on such an enterprise, seeing that it could only hinder their own plans for getting away, and would probably make it much more difficult for them to leave at all, as the Turkish authorities would be sure to take a good deal of trouble to prevent our getting out of the country ; but they seemed to have a profound contempt for any number of gendarmes and no doubt considered we should form a good introduction for them to Russia. Whatever their reasons, it was a very plucky act for four of them to take on a guard of nine, although at the time when the man in black was bowled over it seemed a horribly cold-blooded business.

## CHAPTER XIII

### IN HIDING WITH THE TURKS

THROUGHOUT the following weeks our new friends did all they could to make us as comfortable as circumstances would permit, and we can never be sufficiently grateful to them for thus enabling us to leave captivity and reach home. They would never listen to any offers of payment, saying they did not wish to be taken for men who had rescued us for money.

Going back to the morning of our first acquaintance, we left the guard standing in the road while we, with all their ammunition and four of their rifles, retraced our steps along the road towards the sea and then branched off down a side track, finding a secure hiding-place in a thick wood about a mile further on. We thought it might be as well to impress the guard with the idea that we had been taken off by the " brigands " against our will, and therefore got them to tie our hands together and behaved as if we did not want to go with them at all. When out of sight, we undid the cords and marched on again as really free men, Bihgar Bey continually cheering us by saying, " Allons, enfants de la patrie," which, considering his position as an outlaw, was distinctly humorous. It was wonderful the inspiring effect the change from captivity had upon Tip., who had been so seedy during the last few days ; now he began to recover rapidly and succeeded in marching all the following night without any ill effects.

We had taken Sweet's kit with us, thinking we might meet him and that in any case it would be of no use to leave it with the guard. After sorting it out, we took one or two articles each and made our rescuers some small presents from the remainder. Bihgar and Kiarmil went off to fill our water-bottles and returned a little while later, after announcing their approach by clapping their hands. This we found was the method always adopted by the akhardash when meeting each other in woods or by night.

It was arranged that two of them would accompany us down at nightfall to a secure hiding-place, while the other two were to go in the opposite direction to meet friends from Boiabad who were also joining the party and, as far as we could make out, were bringing a good deal of money with them. In the end, we set off about half-past seven under the guidance of Keor, the old Armenian, while the other three set off again towards Boiabad. They had told us that we should reach our hiding-place in three hours, Bihgar Bey making our mouths water by describing it as a place of milk and honey, where we would be provided with meat, butter, eggs and cheese, all of which since we left Kastamuni had seemed the greatest luxuries.

Keor started off at a trot down a path through the wood. He was carrying his own rifle and one of our late guard's weapons, as well as four bandoliers full of ammunition and a bag on his back. We three each carried a rifle, but hoped there would be no more cold-blooded shooting of the type that had effected our rescue. Keor's pace must have been about five miles an hour, and we soon had to request him to go slower, as I had a dicky knee which would be likely to give trouble going downhill at a trot over a bad path with daylight almost gone. Our packs with some of Sweet's kit were now a good weight, so that with a rifle in addition we were well loaded. After being told that we should reach our goal in three hours we felt fairly confident of attaining it in five, especially as we kept up a good pace and the recognized halts were not observed. Keor several times missed his way, but always found it in the end. After a couple of hours we reached a river and wended our weary way down its bed, first on one side, then crossing to the other side and then back again. There was no path and we floundered along amongst the boulders in the darkness. Whenever we halted, which was not often, Keor always said it was now only one hour's march further.

About 3 a.m. we were going along a rough track beside the river bed when suddenly my bad knee gave way and I took a complete toss, rifle and pack going all over the place. There was nothing for it but to go on, so tying up the knee with a puttee, I hobbled on—the others nobly helping me by carrying my rifle. We were now all pretty well done and signs of dawn began to show in the east. Keor was very anxious to get in, saying there would be a great many gendarmes hereabouts the following day. At length we left the river, climbed a small rise, and passed close to some cottages, where the usual dogs soon started a chorus. This led to one or two shots being fired, probably with the idea of scaring off robbers, but, apparently, we were not actually seen. Finally, we dragged ourselves up a steep track, and got to ground in a thick copse. We were worn out ; it was now a quarter-past five and we had done nine and a quarter hours instead of the three we had been promised. Still, we were free—and nothing else mattered. We put on what extra garments we had and were very soon asleep.

A few hours later Keor disappeared and returned shortly afterwards with what seemed to us a splendid breakfast : fried eggs, chapatties and yoghourt. Apparently, we were close to the house of an akhardash, from whom all this had been procured. Although some children came near us during the day, we were not discovered, and remained quietly where we were till nightfall. Then we tramped off once more, but only to halt at a very short distance further on under some trees near a house, which was probably the one our breakfast had come from. Here we were met by a boy of fifteen, by name Aziz, who came to us through the trees with a loaded rifle slung over his shoulder. Our friends always carried their rifles with a round in the chamber, but with the bolt not pushed home. We were continually expecting some accident

to happen from this practice, but luckily
nothing did.

Of the rifles belonging to our four rescuers,
two were short Lee-Enfields which had been
captured on the Gallipoli peninsula, and had
found their way to the bazaar in Constantinople, where they had been retailed for £T.10
or nine pounds sterling : now, however, they
assured us that the price had gone up to
£T.20. Musa had a Turkish Mauser, made in
Germany, while Keor possessed a Russian
rifle. Aziz met us with an old Greek weapon,
but much to his delight was given one of the
rifles which had belonged to our guard. He
was a very bright boy, and intensely excited
and jubilant over our rescue and the dis-
comfiture of the guard. In every case, the
muzzle piece was removed so as to lighten
the weapon, a bayonet, apparently, not being
considered worth carrying when fighting gendarmes in the mountains. In addition to
their rifles, some of our friends carried Caucasian daggers. These are straight, with a
very fine sharp point and double-edged blade
about fifteen inches long. They were used
for cutting brushwood, rigging up shelters
in the woods, killing sheep, or chopping up
meat, as required. Whenever we halted,
Keor used to spend much loving care over

his bandoliers of ammunition, seeing that each round was clean and not too loose in its leather loop.

After a few minutes under the trees a woman brought us a frugal supper, after which we set off accompanied by Aziz to find a hiding-place for the following day. A short distance brought us to a small Turkish house where a good deal of conversation took place between Keor, Aziz and the owner. Finally, we were taken into a maize-field and camped under a tree in the centre. The maize was seven or eight feet in height, so that we were well concealed. Our host brought us some bedding, consisting of a couple of old mattresses and quilts. During the following days we had a pretty thorough experience of the delights of such bedding, and came to the conclusion in the end that we should have been happier without any. However, in the present case it was not so bad and we had a comparatively undisturbed night. In the morning food was brought us by our host, which consisted mostly of a vegetable stew and coarse bread. The day was uneventful.

We spent another night in this field and moved on once more the following evening. Keor declared it would only take us half an hour and I trusted it might not be far, as my knee was not much better yet. It amused us to think what a trio of crocks we seemed to be. Tip had been ill off and on most of the time since we left Kastamuni. K. had been very unwell that day and suffered a good deal on account of his short sight ; and I was dead lame. A few minutes after starting we met another of the akhardash, a very good fellow named Kasim, and conversed with him for a few minutes in the shade of a corn stack before proceeding.

It was a fine moonlight night, and we again passed the German wireless station, which was now below us and between us and the sea. In not more than an hour, we got close to the place appointed and after a long wait were conducted to a spot which seemed very secure, as it was in the centre of a thick copse with no houses near. Another youth turned up here and, apparently, was the son of our new host. For the next three days we stayed here, this boy bringing us food twice a day and telling Keor all the local news. It was now we heard that Sweet had been retaken or had had to give himself up and was being marched back to Kastamuni. Later when Bihgar Bey and the others rejoined us they declared that Sweet had gone back with an escort of no less than 60 gendarmes. The idea of such a number being necessary tickled them immensely and they evidently considered it a great compliment to the disturbance they had caused, though they were genuinely sorry for Sweet and would have made an effort to rescue him had it been possible.

Our menu was rendered more attractive now by our being able to get a little butter and some fruit. As we had to keep still all day, there was little to do except speculate as to the composition of the next meal, and with having only two meals a day there was a considerable interval between these events. K. spent some time in making up his diary and checking dates. Our friends could never make out what he was writing about, and would say, " Here there are trees and mountains but whatever can a man find to write about ? " Indeed, they never could make K. out very well. Tip was far the most popular; for one thing the fact that he was an aviator roused their imagination, and in addition his good humour under all circumstances made him a great favourite. They always addressed him as Kaptan, but only called K. and me, by our surnames. The want of tobacco in the early days had not affected K. and me, as we did not smoke, but Tip had had to go very short ; now, however, the akhardash seemed to have inexhaustible supplies and were always ready to roll cigarettes for Tip —an art which he never succeeded in mastering. One day Keor informed us that some of the akhardash including Aziz had raided the German wireless station the night before, killing all the Germans and taking a lot of money. This was absolutely untrue, but he seemed to believe it and had evidently been told the story by the boy bringing our food.

# CHAPTER XIV

## CONTINUED DELAYS

ON the afternoon of September 2nd, the third day in this wood, Bihgar Bey and Musa arrived, and announced that the friends from Boiabad had also come and that we should move on towards the sea. One of the new-comers had arrived with them at our lair, this being a stout fellow whom we always referred to as the Fat Boy : he was in fact the only pure Turk amongst them, the others all being of Circassian extraction. As it grew dark we moved off picking up some others of the akhardash shortly afterwards, and took a line which would bring us towards the coast while at the same time approaching Sinope. After some hours, it became evident that they were not very sure of the way, with the result that in the early hours of the morning they decided to stop where they were and reach the appointed place the following evening. At dawn a countryman stumbled upon a sentry guarding a path near which we lay.   He was thoroughly scared and was allowed to go, after having evidently sworn never to tell of anything he had seen.

As morning dawned, rain came on and we moved under some bigger trees, where Keor very soon had a shelter rigged up, cutting down ash saplings with a dagger and using our sail as a cover.  It was not a very efficient protection, but better than nothing and luckily on this occasion the rain did not last long.   Next evening, under the guidance of a new comrade, we were conducted a little way further, finally halting in a maize-field until such time as some unwelcome guests had left our new host.   This was an old Greek as poor as he was dirty, but he had evidently agreed to hide us until the boat was ready and we were much indebted to him.   Finally, the Turkish visitors left the old man and he came to meet us.   The first thing he did was to go off with one of the akhardash and procure a sheep for us.   We had not tasted any meat for about ten days, and looked with great interest at the fine animal now procured.   The old man then brought us bedding, and we are not likely ever to forget it.   We remained in his care for nearly a week, and every day seemed to increase the interest which these mattresses took in us. At daylight, the old man cleared a space for us in a neighbouring thicket, and we moved in there. All the others except Bihgar departed, saying they were going to prepare food for the voyage. Left alone with Bihgar the time hung somewhat heavily. He looked after us like a father and by our calling him this he was highly delighted. He played picquet with Tip, and did his best to learn a little English. The old Greek sent a messenger into Sinope for us, and we thus got hold of a few small note books and some playing cards, which helped to pass the time.

After a few days in our first clearing, we moved to another, a short distance off, this being considered rather safer. There were a good many houses round about and people passed by a path running within 50 yards of where we lay, so that we had to keep very quiet. After three or four days here we began to get a little impatient, Bihgar Bey being somewhat indefinite ; but at last one night, after going off at dark to meet some of the others, he came back and woke us up at midnight and told us to hurry up, as we were off. We hoped we might get right down to the coast andfind the boat ready, but this was not to be. After a second meeting under the tree in the

BICHAR BEY

maize-field and a farewell to the old Greek, we set off down a lane and past some houses where the inevitable dog was soon aroused. However, no one came out and we got out to a field near the main road, where, after a wait of an hour, we were met by Kiarmil, whom we had not seen since the first day. At this point, the others had also met us and had with them a pony laden with bread and a little cheese, which were to be our rations on the voyage. The party now consisted of twelve of the akhardash and a boy with the pony, the latter not intending to leave the country with us.

We learnt that they had had a long fight with the gendarmes the day before, one being killed on each side. Apparently, the gendarmes had rounded them up in a village where they were preparing the food which they had now brought. There were, they said, 80 gendarmes, whereas they had only eight ! Anyhow, our guide of a few nights before, a swarthy, powerful looking man, had been killed, but in the end they had succeeded in getting away from the gendarmes or driving them off. The story, naturally, lost nothing in the telling and we never quite knew what to believe. At first, from their accounts, it sounded as if they had deliberately invited a scrap, and it was some time before we found out that they had been almost surrounded. They also brought the news that hundreds of gendarmes were being sent to Sinope from Kastamuni, but as there were never many at Kastamuni we were somewhat sceptical about this also. Crossing the main road, we found we were close to the sea, and a little further on entered a copse where we spent the rest of the night. At dawn we went still further in, and sentries were posted. Meanwhile, the pony boy had gone off on his steed to Sinope to interview the boatman, and we waited till the afternoon, hoping that we might hear the boat was coming to pick us up that night. Our hopes were dashed again when the boy returned with the news that the boat and its proprietor were not in Sinope, but had gone round the coast to the next port to the west.

The akhardash decided it was too risky to stay where we were and, therefore, we moved again at nightfall. After following the main road a little way on towards Sinope we left it, climbing slowly and going farther away from the sea. After some hours they found that they had missed the way again, although we were close to our destination, which was the inevitable akhardash's house.

Making across some fields and hedges, we gained a lane, but soon had to leave this, as carts were heard coming along. Luckily, Turkish carts make their presence known a long way off by their perpetual creaking, so that we were all safely under cover by the time they passed. A certain amount of misunderstanding now arose, Bihgar not seeing eye to eye with another of the akhardash who knew best our whereabouts, with the result that we nearly split up into two or more groups in the darkness.

However, we eventually all got together again, and reached the house of our new host or rather the field surrounding it. He came to meet us and escorted us to a wood close by. Here we slept till dawn and then moved farther into the trees. This old man was evidently a more influential " comrade " than most of those we had met so far. His house was a good deal larger than the average and he was treated with great respect. Another more humble supporter also appeared, and between the two we were provided with food. Late in the day, the old man departed for Sinope, and our hopes again ran high that he would be successful in arranging for the boat. Disappointment was once more in store for us on his return about six o'clock.

The leading three or four conferred apart with him, and it was not until afterwards that we were told that the Turks were so bent on preventing us leaving the country that they had had all boats pulled up, masts and sails taken out and guarded, and that no boat was allowed to put to sea from Sinope to east-wards of Kusafet, the place where we had been recaptured. The akhardash said that, this being the case, we must try elsewhere, and they proposed to march off towards Iyenjak, a little town about 30 miles westwards, where the restrictions imposed at Sinope would probably not be in force and where they hoped to get another boat. They said if this failed they would then go east to-wards Samsun, a distance of fully 100 miles across rough mountainous country.

We were beginning to wonder if they ever would get afloat. On August 27th, when they had rescued us, they declared every-thing would be ready in three or four days. It was now September and our early sailing seemed more unlikely than ever. In addition to this our boots were nearly worn out, and physically we were not in particularly good condition. It looked as if they would have a much better chance of getting off without us, so we decided to offer to go off on our own and leave them free. We explained that it was a hanging matter for them if caught, whereas it only meant a few months in prison for us. They realized this only too clearly, but would not hear of our leaving them for an instant, and declared they would get a boat, however much it might cost.

Kiarmil, upon whose person all the wealth of the party had been concealed in various places when it was thought we were about to embark, now began to disgorge his treasure and divide it up again. Musa appeared to be by far the richest of the party and seemed to be quite a country gentleman. He told us he would lose his house, cattle and land worth thousands of pounds. These would all be confiscated by the Turkish authorities, but he confidently hoped with the next change of Government to return to the country and get it all back again with a little more besides. Some of the others were in a similar situation in a lesser degree. They had succeeded in changing most of their money into Russian notes which had somehow found their way into Sinope and Jerse, and these transactions had delayed their preparations a good deal.

After a supper which included a little meat and was therefore noteworthy in itself, we set off again on the march, but found we had left behind one of our party who had had fever. At the start, we made good progress along a road, but then turned off to follow a river down the valley. To find the track was not always easy. Many fences had to be partially demolished to allow the pony to get through, and no effort was ever made to repair the damage or conceal our tracks. After crossing a good deal of cultivated land, we reached the river bed and began the type of march we knew so well, crossing continually from one side to the other, stumbling along over boulders and rocks. About three o'clock in the morning, we reached a thicket in a lonely part of the valley where the sides had narrowed considerably. They decided to halt here till the next night, much to our relief. Cross-country marching by night is never a very easy mode of progression, but when an attempt is made to use a stony river bed as a road it becomes a prolonged torture.

No incident marked the following day, and just before dark we were off once more. As dawn was breaking we reached the neighbourhood of yet another akhardash's house and went into hiding in thick brushwood which was soaking with dew. Just as we had got settled down, Bihgar for some reason

decided that we three would be safer elsewhere, and much to our disgust hustled us
off to an equally wet spot in a thicket on the
opposite side of the road.  He was always
prone to worry and fuss a great deal more
than the others, and later on in the day, in
a rash moment, I expostulated with him,
going through a little pantomime to show how
he had acted in the morning.  The effect
was startling and a great deal more than I had
bargained for.  He began by fervently kissing
my hand, declaring he was our servant and
that everything he did was for our benefit.
I hastened to stop the flood of protest and
affection which I had unwittingly let loose,
but it was some time before he was calm again.

That evening we moved on, having been
fed during the day by the local akhardash.
We were now under the command of the
fellow we termed the Fat Boy, Bihgar having
gone off with some of the others to interview
another friend regarding a boat.  This man
never worried at all, and would shout to men
on guard over the crops as if he were a countryman returning home late.  The fires all
over the countryside at night in this district
were used for scaring wild pig from the maize
and other crops.  In nearly every field would
be a small perch for a man, who would keep

a blaze going beside him and make various noises to scare off the intruders. Most of them had old guns of some sort and frequently a shot would be heard. The subject of pig formed a perpetual joke ; the akhardash, as Mussulmans, declaring it was not good to eat, whereas we always offered to show them how good it was if they would bring us one. Another source of never-ending merriment was the prophecy that Tip would be taken prisoner when flying in France and again be sent to Kastamuni.

Towards midnight we reached a big wood and, under the guidance of a new supporter, found a sheltered spot beneath lofty trees. The character of the country had altered a good deal since we had reached the coast. Here the rainfall was evidently a great deal heavier than it was at Kastamuni and the climate milder, with the result that all sorts of trees abounded and the vegetation was much thicker. This was the first spot considered safe enough by our friends for a fire and they soon had a fine blaze going. We lay down in the warmth and were quickly asleep. Our comfort was short-lived, however, as it began to rain heavily. A small oil silk sheet which had belonged to Sweet kept me dry for a time, but it soon became

necessary to move, as the fire had nearly gone
out and another had been started further
away. Tip evinced a wonderful power of
being able to sleep when lying in a puddle
and soaked through. The akhardash were
experts at fire-lighting, under all circumstances, and skilfully arranged the logs to
protect the inside of the blaze from the rain.

In the afternoon we moved on under the
guidance of two sturdy lads, one of whom with
the aid of an axe cut a way for us through
the brushwood and made a track up the steep
hill, along which the pony struggled heroic-
ally. On reaching higher ground we found
a path and followed this a little further to a
water trough, near which we camped, another
fire being lighted at once. Our guide of the
night before turned out to be a Turkish
soldier on leave, but he showed little surprise
on finding out who we were. The other
lads had also been in the Army and, as far
as we could make out, had been sent to their
homes on account of the shortage of rations in
Constantinople. They bore us no ill will and
evidently thought that the Gallipoli campaign
showed them to be the better soldiers of the two.
They knew nothing about our having taken
Bagdad and were quite ignorant of all other
war news. The following day was fine at

intervals, generally just long enough to allow of our drying our clothes before it began again. Our diet had been limited to coarse Turkish bread, of a most indigestible and half-baked variety, with potatoes and meat which we cooked by toasting small pieces on long sticks ; but now the bread ran out and for two days we lived almost entirely on potatoes. The erstwhile soldiers also brought us a number of small pears. For washing we had the trough, but while the rain continued and for some time after each shower a small stream flowed down beside our camp.

The next event of interest was the arrival of a visitor who brought with him a sheep. We were told that this man had been employed in the *gendarmerie*, but was now also leaving for Russia and intended to sail in ten days' time. He suddenly wanted our party to postpone their departure, so that he might join us, but this was not agreed to. To show his good faith, he had brought the sheep as a present and no time was lost in turning it into mutton. A long pole was cut and supported horizontally on two Y pieces driven into the ground beside the fire. The sheep's carcase was scientifically balanced and tied to the pole and the roasting process then began, the pole being slowly turned in the supports. We made use of our canteens and anything else we could get hold of to catch the dripping : butter had been scarce and any substitute was greatly in demand. Our experience in this connection was that coarse indigestible bread became much less harmful when any butter could be had to eat with it.

# CHAPTER XV

T HERE had been a certain amount of going and coming amongst the akhardash during the days we spent in this wood, but on September 19th Bihgar Bey arrived and declared everything was arranged. A boat said to be quite new had been purchased for 400 liras. This sum had been paid in hard cash, gold and silver, a fact of more interest than might appear since at this time not a single coin of any description was to be seen in the bazaars in Turkey. Notes had been issued down to 1 piastre and below this postage stamps were used. We again offered to contribute a share to the cost of the boat, but they would not hear of it. Nearly all of them had some gold coins, English sovereigns being as numerous as Turkish lira pieces. The following day, September 20th, our gendarme friend again appeared, bringing another sheep, which was cooked without delay in the same manner as the first. We were to leave that evening at six o'clock, go down to the coast and embark the following evening. At last everything seemed to have been definitely arranged and our spirits rose accordingly.

A dark night march followed over some bad going and as we got lower down we entered the inevitable river bed. This lasted for an hour only and we then climbed a hill and found ourselves in a small copse immediately above the sea.

Since our recapture at the coast we reckoned we had covered about 150 miles, while our trek from Kastamuni to the coast must have been about 200 miles.

In the morning the pony boy was sent along to interview the boat owner, and on his return we were told the boat was to come along at dark and we were to embark at eleven o'clock. The day passed uneventfully, and there was nothing to be done but to lie still and hope that no misfortune would upset the scheme at the last moment. On these occasions the akhardash posted one or more sentries round our hiding-place and great care was taken to make no noise. As it grew dark Bihgar told us to go to sleep and said he would awaken us when the boat came. No sign of the boat had been seen and they were evidently

P

much worried.   It looked as if even now something had gone wrong.   The pony boy was despatched again, and returned hours later to say that the boat had left as arranged.

Meanwhile, we had gone to sleep and did not wake until dawn.   An awful presentiment seized us that another failure had occurred. However, as it grew light, the sentries who had not seen the boat the night before discovered it a quarter of a mile away across a stream with a fire lit on the beach above it. This had, apparently, been the signal, but for some reason had not been seen.   No time was now lost in getting down to the boat. The pony boy galloped off, presumably to his home, and we trust never aroused the suspicions of the authorities.   The sacks containing the bread for the voyage were carried down and put on board, and a kerosine tin and keg from the boat taken to the stream to provide the water supply.   Meanwhile, others had been ballasting the boat with boulders from the beach.   Just as the water was being brought back to the boat an old sentry emerged from a tumble-down house on the beach, which our friends had, apparently, thought to be deserted.   He had scarcely taken in the situation before he was disarmed and tied up near the house.   His Mauser

BOAT IN WHICH THE PARTY CROSSED THE BLACK SEA

rifle and ammunition were all taken from him, and in exchange he was left with an old Greek rifle, but without a round to put in it. The last of the party pushing off the boat leaped on board, and with thankful hearts we felt we really were off at last. Our vessel was the usual type of coastal fishing boat, with a single big sail. She was about twenty-four feet long and between two or three tons displacement, but, whereas we had been expecting a new boat, we now found a very old one with mast and rigging that looked anything but trustworthy, the only sign of any recent attention being a little fresh paint here and there. However, we had left Turkey and had a boat and that was all we wanted. The question of navigation and handling the boat we left to start with to the akhardash, of whom several said they were accustomed to sailing and knew all about it ; but we relied on Tip's experience to help us along if our other friends failed.

The first thing that engaged our attention, when the boat had been pushed off, was another vessel of the same type which was very slowly making its way close in along the coast and was now quite near to us. The result of a short palaver amongst the akhardash was that they rowed quietly up to this boat, not a rifle showing and all except the four rowers sitting down as quiet as mice. On getting up to the new-comer they all jumped up and levelled their rifles at the unfortunate crew in true pirate style. The crew had no course left but to accept any orders they were given, and after a few minutes' violent yelling and gesticulation their captain and one other were transferred to our boat, while Musa and the Fat Boy took their places in the other. Both boats now sailed off in company. There was a good breeze from the east and they had decided to make for Sevastopol ; but it soon became evident that they had little idea of the direction as a course N.E. was taken, whereas Sevastopol lay rather to the west of the point at which we left the coast. Other diversions, however, put questions of direction in the background for some time. To start with, the spar in our boat very nearly broke in two and had to be lowered and patched with two small pieces of wood and some old nails, a makeshift which gave little promise of being a permanent remedy. This was not accomplished without a tremendous hulla-baloo, in which Bihgar played a prominent part. Arms were waving and all seemed to be yelling instructions to all the others.

During the process the end of the rope

suspending the spar ran through the pulley at the top of the mast, and it became necessary to get it back again somehow. The captured captain of the second boat made a noble effort, swarming up the mast and holding on to the shrouds like a monkey ; but the boat was rocking about a good deal and after several vain attempts he had to give it up. This necessitated the mast being unshipped and causing more frantic excitement, especially when the moment arrived to put it up again. But, in the end, the feat was successfully accomplished and both boats sailed off in company. The breeze was strong and the sea choppy. Several of the akhardash at once became *hors de combat* and remained nearly motionless at the bottom of the boat for the next three days. It was a glorious morning, and, as we watched the coast receding, we were more than repaid for all the discomfort of the last few weeks. The Sinope headland stood out away on our right, and it was not till late in the afternoon that we were out of sight of the mountains. A small boat crossed our course soon after starting, but there were no signs of any pursuit or commotion on shore. We wondered what stories of our doings would reach our friends in Kastamuni, and were pretty sure that the Turks would tell them we had come to an unhappy end at the hands of the " brigands."

We now attempted to get our friends to steer a course more nearly north instead of north-east ; but they would not do so, as they were in a terrible state of apprehension lest they should reach Rumanian territory occupied by Germans. K. produced our chart—the largest map of the Black Sea we had been able to find at Kastamuni—but it was only some three or four inches long and coming as it did from an " Ancient Atlas " showed the Greek colonies in 500 B.C. and nothing more modern. We were not sure of the exact position of Sevastopol but did not allow our friends to know. Whatever was urged had no effect and the course remained N.E.

When dark came on, it soon became evident that neither our captured mariners nor the akhardash had the least idea of steering by the stars ; and, finally, about midnight, Tip discovered we were going about due east. We thought it was high time we took charge, and therefore arranged to take watches, one of us sitting up beside the steersman and keeping the direction a little west of north. The boat had no cabin, but the stern was decked across and we were allowed to keep this to ourselves.

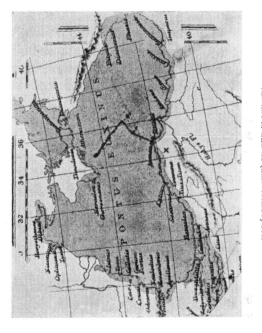

MAP (ACTUAL SIZE) OF THE BLACK SEA

All the first day there had been a good breeze, but it became much feebler at night. With dawn the wind grew stronger again, and we were making a good pace in company with the second boat when, at nine o'clock, signals of distress from her were noticed. She was about 300 yards from us at the time and it was impossible to make out what had happened. Pandemonium at once reigned on board and we thought by the commotion that our companion must be sinking. After much shouting, our sail was lowered, the oars got out and the vessel slowly brought up to our comrade in distress, only to find that the latter had broken her rudder. Much shouting now took place on both sides. Any thought of steering with an oar was never entertained and they decided to abandon one boat. As the captured second boat was so much the better of the two, an attempt was made to substitute our rudder in her, but without success. The result was that she was abandoned after transferring her crew, sail and spar, and part of her cargo to our boat. We were now packed very tightly, having a total of nineteen on board. Some of the ballast had been thrown overboard, but not enough to compensate for the additional load. Had we realized at the time that the second boat had a valuable cargo of kerosine, the price of which was fabulous in Turkey, we should have made some attempt to salve her or, at all events, have set her on fire. This information was not divulged till afterwards, but even so it is doubtful if she would not have sunk before drifting ashore or being discovered by another boat.

All went well, despite the crowd, until about midday, when the wind dropped altogether and rowing had to be resorted to. The boat was arranged for four oars and it was in this capacity that the captured crew proved of the greatest service. They were relieved at intervals by some of the akhardash. We calculated our speed when rowing at about two miles an hour, whereas for the first 24 hours it must have been at least double this. I plotted our course as nearly as possible on the diminutive map, and it was annoying to see how much further on we should have been had we started in the right direction the day before.

Our rations were the coarse bread, together with a little honey and butter which we had preserved for some days ; but as neither of the latter could be said to be good they were not of much value. Some of our Horlick's milk was still left, and this helped matters along.

The morning of the third day broke with windless serenity and rowing went on uninterruptedly. The sky was perfectly clear, but at midday we noticed some very small clouds straight ahead which seemed stationary. We held on our course, trusting that the clouds meant land. At 6 o'clock that morning, as far as we could make out from the chart, we were at least seventy miles from the nearest point of the Crimea.

During the afternoon the question of rations and water was discussed, and we decided that if land was not in sight the next morning to take over all the remaining bread and water and distribute it ourselves, as the akhardash had not the least idea of rationing and used to eat and drink as the inclination prompted them. We had not liked to interfere before, but now it was a matter of necessity.

The sun set in a glorious blaze, and just at this moment there was a commotion at the forward end of the boat and the word went round that land was sighted. It was anything but clear, but we took the word of the sailors for it and every one became much excited. Just before this event, Keor had made a fire in the bottom of the boat, making a hearth with some of the stone ballast and using some floor boards and any other bits of wood he could find as fuel. On this was cooked some meal which had been brought in from the abandoned boat ; sea water was used to boil it and a very useful sort of porridge resulted.

# CHAPTER XVI

## THE CRIMEA AND HOME

AT dawn on the fourth day, September 25th, the land was very clear and we could see a lofty headland which ran steeply down to the sea. An hour or two later, we could make out houses and then it became clear that we were approaching some seaside resort. All through the previous two days, after we had taken charge of the steering, the akhardash had continually inquired whether the " road " was " good " and they were now more than satisfied that we knew the best way over the sea. Fortune had been with us, in giving us fine weather and clear skies by day and night ; otherwise we might have reached a very different destination. Rowing on steadily, it was soon clear that the place was quite extensive and probably much frequented. Several large buildings could be seen and something which looked like a pier or jetty, to which we now steered. It was not until one o'clock that we finally reached this spot and landed, to find ourselves opposite the baths.

For days we had talked of the delights of a good hot bath and now we had come straight to the very place. We were met by a Swiss who was bathing. He hurried off to dress, but before he could return we were accosted by several other people, notably a retired Russian general and an American diplomat who lent us clothes and escorted us to the baths. After getting really clean once more, we were taken to a *pension* and made the guests of the hospitable Russian ladies to whom it belonged. They told us the place was called Alupka and was one of the most popular seaside places in Russia. Meanwhile the akhardash had been escorted into the town. In the morning they had begun to don their bandoliers and handle their rifles, but we persuaded them that they would be looked upon in a more friendly manner on landing if they abandoned these weapons.

It had taken us 78 hours to cross the 180 miles of sea, but actually we must have sailed well over 200 miles. We found that, comparing our position on the third morning with the spot we had marked on the map, we were only some twenty miles out, which, as amateur navigators, we considered quite good work.

АЛУПКА

THE ALUPKA BATHS

At the *pension* we were given lunch, and wine was produced in our honour by our new friends.   We shall never forget their kindness, and the extraordinary feeling of being amongst all the amenities of civilization once more after two years under other conditions.   In the afternoon, we were taken to the municipal office and there interviewed by a very business-like and intelligent lady who seemed to combine the duties of commissioner of police and most other municipal departments.   Our friends told us that there was some difficulty in establishing our identity, since the commandant of the town—who a few months earlier before the Revolution had been an actor—was very suspicious and inclined to believe we were really Germans.   In fact, some splendid stories were going about. According to one, a boat-load of Turks under the command of three German officers had attacked the town, one of the Germans being wounded.   Tip had been to see a doctor and this no doubt lent colour to the idea. At all events, the commandant told off a sentry to shadow us about wherever we went.

The akhardash, we found, had been accommodated in the central police building, where they had been given plenty of food and seemed to be receiving visitors.   We bought them some fruit and tried to cheer them up, as they had imagined they would be received with triumphal rejoicings and were somewhat crestfallen at being treated more like prisoners. Our first object was to get in touch with the nearest British consul, so as to put their case before him and get matters explained to the Russian authorities ; but no one seemed to know where the nearest consul was to be found. We got telegrams sent off to our people at home addressed to the Embassy at Petrograd. It was hopeless at this time to try to get private telegrams through, and for mails from home we found they were even worse off here than we had been in Kastamuni. It was strange, indeed, being in a spick and span town, with well made roads and everything clean and up-to-date, after the filthy dilapidation which characterizes everything in connection with the Turk.

Some people we met seemed rather annoyed that we had not struck a mine, as they assured us there was a large minefield through which we had passed. We discovered, later, this was quite wrong, but in any case our boat was of much too shallow draft to be in much danger. Others told us that we were fortunate to land where we did, as had we gone a little further east we should have come to the estates of some of the Grand Dukes who at that time were interned under armed guards, with orders to prevent anyone approaching from land or sea ! We were told that every one was on rations and that food was getting scarce. One of the most striking contrasts to Turkey was the magnificent fruit on sale, grapes, pears and peaches, all evidently cultivated with great skill.

As we emerged from our interview with the lady commissioner, we were summoned to halt in order to be cinematographed by the representatives of some Moscow firm. All the educated people we met in Russia were kindness itself to us and made our journey through the country very pleasant. It was pathetic to be asked, as we were, to tell people in England that not every one in Russia is bad and worthless. All classes, we found, had welcomed the Revolution when it started, thinking a new and brighter era had dawned ; but it very soon became clear that the pendulum was swinging much too far in the other direction, and no one would dare to prophesy what might happen next. Fortunately for us, there was no actual internal fighting taking place at the time and we got through the country without trouble.

The following day we left Alupka by motor

for Yalta, a port a little further east. The
road led past some of the Grand Dukes' estates
and Livadia, the Tsar's Crimean palace. The
scenery all along was magnificent, the pine-
clad hillsides sloping steeply down to the blue,
with white houses or palaces. Yalta itself was
one of the most charming spots it had been
our good fortune to see, and is easily equal in
beauty to any of the Riviera resorts. From
here we were to travel by night by a transport
back past Alupka, reaching Sevastopol on the
following morning, but before leaving a
surprise was in store for us. As we had some
time to wait, we went into an hotel, with the
officer conducting us, for tea. This, however,
we found was the headquarters of the local
committee of soldiers and workmen, and a
few minutes later we were asked to go into
their meeting hall to receive their congratula-
tions. This promised to be rather awkward,
as we knew no word of Russian ; but fortunately a schoolmaster who knew French was
introduced to us. As we entered the room,
the soldiers and sailors present all clapped
vigorously. There were about 30 or 40
present and it was necessary, as on every
possible occasion in Russia, to shake hands
all round. The schoolmaster then gave a
harrowing account of our imprisonment in

YALTA

Turkey and told them how we had eventually escaped and reached Russia. He appeared to say that we had been manacled in chains and endured the worst possible fortune as prisoners. After a suitable expression of thanks conveyed through the schoolmaster, we shook hands again all round and returned to our tea. This was our only actual meeting with a revolutionary committee, and we are bound to say they seemed to have no love for the Turk or any wish to leave their Allies in the lurch by concluding a separate peace.

The transports steamed only at night and kept close into the coast for fear of possible submarines ; so that the chances of our being picked up by one on our way over had been very remote.

The akhardash travelled with us to Sevastopol, and on arrival there we met the British Naval Representative, Commander Sage, R.N., who looked after us for the next few days. As he spoke Russian fluently and was in touch with all the highest authorities, we had no trouble of any sort. The akhardash were handed over to the Russian Staff authorities, who provided them with good quarters on a ship in the harbour. We three lived with Commander Sage on an auxiliary cruiser, the *Almaz*, which had previously been

Q

used as a private yacht by the Grand Dukes.
The akhardash had for some time wished that
we should all be photographed together and
we, too, were anxious to have such mementoes
of our time with them. The Russian Staff
very kindly arranged it and we had two groups
taken, one with our original rescuers with
their rifles and bandoliers, and one with all
the others included. Unfortunately Keor,
the old Armenian, was ill in hospital and could
not be present. As some days had elapsed
before the photos were taken, our friends had
obtained new clothing and hats and, therefore,
did not present the picturesque appearance
to which we had become accustomed. As
regards some recompense for all their services,
we could not get them to accept anything
more than what they had spent on our food
during all the time we were with them, but
the Russians paid them the exact sum they
had given for the boat, so that they were not
out of pocket on that account. As souvenirs,
they had given us each one of their long
Caucasian daggers, and we in return got wrist
watches for them and a suitably inscribed
cigarette case for Bihgar Bey. We left them
in good hands and have often wondered since
what has been their fortune. No men could
have acted more pluckily in rescuing us in

THE THREE OFFICERS AND THREE OF THEIR RESCUERS

the first place, or taken more trouble over our comfort and welfare during the weeks we spent with them in the hills and woods ; and never shall we forget how much we owe them.

After some days in Sevastopol, we said good-bye to them and went round to Odessa on the *Almaz*, where we made arrangements with the British consul for our journey home. At Odessa we were entertained at a most convivial dinner by the British and American Club.   Like all dinners in Russia, it proved prolific in speeches, a start being made with the King's health, in the middle of the fish course, by an enthusiastic American.   From these speeches we learnt how whole-heartedly the great American nation had entered the struggle and the efforts they were making in Russia, more especially with regard to improving the railways.   Coming out of the obscurity of Turkey, these things were new to us, although by reading between the lines of the Turkish papers we had been able to get a fair idea of the general position on the actual battle fronts.   Another speaker told a pitiful story of the position in Rumania and of the appalling lack of medical stores and awful ravages of disease in the Army.   A visit to the races and opera helped to pass two very enjoyable days before saying good-bye to

Commander Sage and our new friends, and leaving for Mogileff, the then headquarters on the Russian front to which we had been summoned by the British Mission.

On our way we passed through Kieff, a magnificent town, peopled very largely by Poles. Here we met some forlorn British gunners who did not know what was to be their fate, but were soon, I trust, back in England. After a day in Mogileff we went on to Petrograd. Travelling even at this time was very comfortable on the Russian lines, for those with passes such as we possessed, except for the temperature of the carriages. In some it was impossible to open any window. The result was that we all got heavy colds, although during the past six weeks we had kept fit while sleeping out in the open and occasionally getting soaked through.

Petrograd was cold, wet, and dreary, and we spent our time in rushing about between the various departments before we could get passports and tickets through to Bergen. We, eventually, accomplished this by hard work in three days, and were then told we were fortunate not to have been kept at it for a week. It was necessary to borrow mufti to travel through Sweden and Norway. Clothes in Russia were practically unobtainable, but, fortunately for us, two naval

THE THREE OFFICERS AND THE AKHARDASH

officers at the Embassy came to our rescue by most generously giving us the necessary garments. We were also indebted to the Red Cross Depot at the Embassy for other assistance in the way of clothes.

Tip and I left on October 14th, and after an interesting trip through Sweden and Norway reached Aberdeen ten days later.

K., on the other hand, returned to the Black Sea. It had been hoped, and we had done our best to arrange, that an attempt should be made with the assistance of the akhardash to release some of the other officers at Kastamuni. Unfortunately this plan never materialized: for one thing our friends were moved further inland from Kastamuni before any attempt could be made, and when everything was settled on our side the Bolshevik rising had commenced and brought all plans to a standstill. K. reached England two months later, after having made a trip over to the Turkish coast in a Russian destroyer, and worked in every conceivable way to bring off the scheme for the rescue of the other officers. His persistent but unsuccessful efforts bring the account of our adventures to a close.

# CHAPTER XVII

## FRIENDS IN CAPTIVITY

THIS story would not be complete without recording the deaths of Captain R. J. Tipton, R.F.C., and Captain R. T. Sweet, D.S.O., 2/7th Ghurka Rifles.

Tipton, after very few days at home, reported again for duty and would not rest content until he had obtained leave to fly and fight over the German lines. For this purpose he had refused his majority. On March 9th he was severely wounded in a fight with a Hun whom he brought down. With great courage and skill he brought his own machine back and landed safely, but the injury he had received proved fatal and he died three days later.

Tipton thus went back to fight at the earliest possible moment, feeling it his duty to the other officers left behind in Turkey, who were bound to be suffering for our escape. Although the youngest of our party, he was our leader on the long journey to the coast ; and to his unfailing good humour and tact we owed much more than we realized at the time. Although in pain for many days, he kept cheerfully on and would never give in.

Few men have been more beloved by all with whom they came in contact, and his gallant death has left a wide blank in the affections of all who had the privilege to know him.

Sweet, whose gallantry at Kut had earned him the D.S.O., was imprisoned at Angora, after being brought back from the coast, and exhibited to the other officers at Kastamuni for a few minutes on the way. He shouted to them to take a few days' provisions and try their luck, that it was quite easy to get away, and that he meant to start again the first chance he had. In reply they cheered him, much to the disgust of the Turks.

After two dreadful months in the civil prison at Angora, he was taken to the officers' camp at Yozgad, a place 4,000 feet above the sea amongst the hills, in the very centre of Asia Minor. Here he remained till a few weeks before the armistice with Turkey was announced, when he fell a victim to the influenza scourge and died of pneumonia.

In our escape Sweet was always the most indefatigable, and on many an occasion spurred us on when we three had no energy left. His knowledge of Turkish was invaluable and enabled us successfully to bluff our way along during the days when we were posing as Germans. It was only the merest accident that parted him from us when the akhardash arrived, and it is hard to feel that so small a thing should have ultimately resulted in the death of such a brave officer.

The first officers who died in Kastamuni were Lieutenants Reynolds, of the 103rd L.I., and Lock, of the I.A.R.O., attached 104th Rifles. Reynolds had been unwell during most of the journey up and, undoubtedly, had not got over the hardships of the siege ; he succumbed within a few days of our arrival. Lock, who had been an indigo planter in Bihar, went down with peritonitis very shortly afterwards. Both officers had done well in Kut and were greatly liked by all who knew them. Their death in a strange country, after the worst of our troubles seemed to be over, was all the sadder to think of.

The third officer who died was Commander Crabtree, R.N.R., of the S.Y. *Zaida*, which struck a mine while patrolling the Adana coast. He, along with three other officers from the same ship, was sent on to Kasta-muni. At Angora he was ill, but the Turks considered him fit enough to travel, and sent him on in a springless country cart over the 140 miles of rough road to Kastamuni. Riding in a cart over this road is bad enough for a fit man, but in his case it must have simply jolted him to death. At all events, he arrived dying, and never regained con-sciousness.

Another sad death occurred amongst the officers after they had been moved to Changri from Kastamuni. On Christmas Day, 1917, Major Corbett, 48th Pioneers, died suddenly from an aneurism of the heart after some strenuous tobogganing, which had been allowed as a special concession.

Major Corbett was one of those officers who assisted our party to escape and would himself have come with us had he considered there was any small chance of success. To the camp at Kastamuni he was invaluable as staff officer to the lower group of houses, always energetic and cheery and turning his hand to something. Carpentry formed his chief occupation when not playing games.

Q*

He was one of those men whom we felt we simply could not do without, and his loss may well be imagined in the camp at Changri, where conditions had been rough and painful in the extreme.

# APPENDIX A

## *GARRISON OF KUT*

### HEADQUARTERS

### MAJOR-GEN. C. V. TOWNSHEND, G.O.C.

16th Infantry Brigade, MAJ.-GEN. DELAMAIN.
- 2nd Dorsets.
- 66th Punjabis.
- 104th Rifles.
- 117th Mahrattas.

17th Infantry Brigade, GEN. HOGHTON.
- Oxford and Bucks L.I.
- 22nd Punjabis.
- 103rd Infantry.
- 119th Infantry.

18th Infantry Brigade, GEN. HAMILTON.
- 2nd Norfolks.
- 120th Infantry.
- 110th Infantry.
- 7th Rajputs.

30th Infantry Brigade, MAJ.-GEN. MELLIS
- 2 Coys. Royal West Kents.
- 3 Coys. 4th Hants T.F.
- 2/7th Ghurka Rifles.
- 24th Punjabis.
- 67th Punjabis.
- 76th Punjabis.

## DIVISIONAL TROOPS

17th Coy., S. & M.

34th (Poona) Signalling Co.

Sirmoor Sappers (Imperial Service).

1 Squadron 7th Hariana Lancers.

48th Pioneers.

63rd, 76th, 82nd Batteries, R.F.A. 18 guns, 18 pdr.

104th Battery, R.G.A. 2 4″ guns.

84th Battery, R.G.A. 4 5″ guns.

Volunteer Battery. 4 15 pdr. guns.

" S " Battery, R.H.A., left behind 2 14 pdr. guns.

Naval Detachment. 4 4·7″ pdr. guns.

H.M.S. *Samarra :* 2 3 pdr. guns ; 1 13 pdr. gun.

Machine Gun Battery (6 guns).

Supply and Transport, including Jeypore Transport Train, Wireless, Royal Flying Corps, Depot and other details.

## MEDICAL SERVICE

One British General Hospital.

One Indian General Hospital.

3 Field Ambulances.

|  | *Strength of garrison at beginning of siege.* | *Strength on surrender.* |
|---|---|---|
| British Officers - - | 301 | 277 |
| British Rank and File | 2,851 | 2,592 |
| Indian Officers - - | 225 | 204 |
| Indian Rank and File | 8,230 | 6,988 |
| Indian Followers - | 3,530 | 3,248 |
| Total - | 15,137 | 13,309 |

Losses: Killed and died of wounds, 1,025.
Died of disease, and missing, 803.
Arab population of Kut (?) 3,700.
Animals (horses and mules) before killing for food, 3,000.

# APPENDIX B

Copy of translation of pamphlets thrown over from Turkish trenches towards our line during the earlier part of the siege and picked up between the two old lines when these had been evacuated on Jan. 21st.

OH DEAR INDIAN BRETHREN,

You understand the fact well that God has created this war for the sake of setting India free from the hands of the cruel English. That is the reason why all the Rajahs and Nawabs with the help of Brave Indian soldiers are at present creating disturbances in all parts of India and are forcing the English out of the country. Consequently not a single Englishman is to be seen in the N.W. Frontier of India districts of Saad, Chakdara, Mohmand and Kohat. Brave Indian soldiers have killed several of their officers at Singapore, Secunderabad and Meerut cantonments. Many of the Indian soldiers have on several occasions joined our allies the Turks, Germans, and Austrians of which you must have heard.

O heroes ! our friends the Turks, Germans and Austrians are trying merely for the freedom of our country (India) from the English and you being Indians are fighting against them thus causing delay. On seeing your degraded position one feels severely ashamed (lit. ' blood in the eyes ') that you have not got fed up of their disgraceful conduct and hatred towards you.

You should remember how cruelly were Maharajah Ranjit Singh of the Punjab and Sultan Tipu treated by the English govt., and now when our beloved country is being released from their cruel clutches you should not delay the freedom of your country and try to restore happiness to the souls of your forefathers as you come from the same heroic generation to which the brave soldiers of the Dardanelles and Egypt belong.

You must have heard about the recent fighting in the Dardanelles when Lord Hamilton was wounded and Lord Kitchener cowardly ran away at night taking with him only the British soldiers from the Dardanelles siege and leaving behind the Indian soldiers who on seeing this murdered all their officers and joined the Turks.

Nearly everywhere we find that our Indian soldiers are leaving the British. Is it not a pity that you still go on assisting them? Just consider that these and we have left our homes and country and are fighting only for rupees fifteen or twenty; a subaltern 20 or 25 years old is drawing a handsome amount as salary from Indian money while our old Risaldar and Subadar majors are paid nothing like him—and even a British soldier does not salute them. Is that all the respect and share of wealth for the sake of which we should let them enjoy our country?

For instance see how many of you Indian soldiers were killed and wounded during the battle of Ctesiphon and there is nobody to look after the families of your deceased and wounded brothers. Just compare the pay a British soldier draws with that which you get. Brethren hurry up, the British Kingdom is going to ruins now. Bulgaria gave them several defeats, Ireland and the Transvaal are out of their possessions of which perhaps you already know.

H.M. the Sultan's brave Turkish forces which were engaged at the Bulgar frontier before are now coming over this side in lacs for the purpose of setting India at liberty.

We were forced by the British to leave our beloved country for good and had to live in America, but on hearing the news of our country being freed from English hands we came here via Germany and found our Indian brethren fighting against H.M. Sultan.

Other nations are trying to restore us freedom from the British, but it appears we do not like to be freed from slavery, hence we are fighting against our friends the Turks.

Brethren, what is done, that is done, and now you should murder all your officers and come over to join H.M. Sultan's Army like our brave Indian soldiers did in Egypt and the Dardanelles. All the officers of this force and Arabs have received orders from the Sultan that any Indian soldier, irrespective of any caste, a Sikh, Rajput, Mahratta, Gurkha, Pathan, Shiah or Syed, who come to join the Turks should be granted a handsome pay and land for cultivation if they like to settle in the Sultan's territory. So you must not miss the chance of murdering your officers and joining the Turks, helping them to restore your freedom.

Dated 28th December, 1915.

Printed and distributed by the Indian National Society.

Translated from originals in Urdu and Pushtu or Punjabi.

# APPENDIX C

Comparison of rations issued in Kut at the middle of April, 1916, with full service rations.

## BRITISH

| *Normal Field Service.* | *In Kut.* |
|---|---|
| Bread, 1¼ lb. | 4 oz. (from April 17th). |
| Fresh meat, 1¼ lb. | 1¼-1½ lb. (horse and mule). |
| Potatoes and vegetables, ½ lb. | Nil. (except ság). |
| Bacon, 3 oz. | Nil. |
| (or butter 1½ oz. twice a week). | |
| Tea, ⅝ oz. | Nil. |
| Sugar, 3 oz. | Nil. |
| Salt, ½ oz. | Nil. |
| Jam, 4 oz. | Nil. |
| Cheese, 3 oz. | Nil. |
| Ginger, — | ⅓ oz. |

## INDIAN

| *Normal Field Service.* | *In Kut.* |
|---|---|
| Atta (wheat meal), 1½ lb. | 4 oz. (barley meal). |
| Ghi, 2 oz. | ½ oz. |
| Dal, 4 oz. | Nil. |
| Meat, 4 oz. | 9 oz. (horse). |
| Gur, 1 oz. | Nil. |
| Potatoes, 2 oz. | Nil. |
| Tea, ⅓ oz. | Nil. |
| Ginger, ⅛ oz. | |
| Chillies, ⅛ oz. | |
| Turmeric, ⅛ oz. | ⅛ oz. |
| Garlic, ⅛ oz. | |
| Salt, ½ oz. | |

# APPENDIX D

All except meat and ginger dropped by aeroplane.

| *British.* | *Indian.* |
| --- | --- |
| Bread, 3 oz. | Indian atta, 3 oz. |
| Sugar, 1 oz. | Gur, $\frac{1}{2}$ oz. |
| Chocolate, $\frac{1}{2}$ oz. | Dal, 1 oz. |
| Meat, $1\frac{1}{2}$ lb. (horse or mule). | Salt, $\frac{1}{8}$ oz. |
| | Ginger, $\frac{1}{8}$ oz. |
| | Meat, 9 oz. (horse). |